How to
Reclaim Your Innocence

Remembering the Love-Beauty Within

Temba Spirit

Temba Spirit

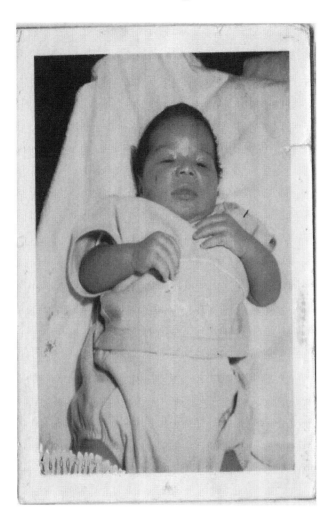

I Adore You just as You are

CRITICAL ACCLAIM

"I believe that this book was Divinely channeled so that those who are about to give up on love open their hearts one more time and experience the pure joy of giving love with no other agenda, those who are about to give up on their brothers and sisters open their eyes one more time and see the spark of good that is in everyone, and those who are about to give up on God look for grace one more time and find that just on the other side of the darkness, the light is waiting to embrace them. Thank you Temba for being such an open vessel for God to work through."

—***Debra Poneman***, *best-selling author Chicken Soup of The American Idol Soul and founder of Yes to Success, Inc.*

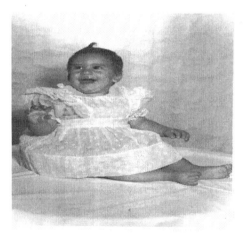

Debra is so Success-Full & also

a Master of the Relative!

"Temba brilliantly and compellingly reminds us of the true power we had as children. He takes us on a journey into the heart, where we reconnect with our child-like innocence and our loving essence."

—*Marci Shimoff, #1 NY Times bestselling author of Love for No Reason and Happy for No Reason*

Marci is so Lovable, Loving & Happy

For No Reason

"Temba Spirit graces us with a vital reminder of that place within us that has never been nor can ever be hurt, harmed, or endangered—the perpetual innocence of our inner spirit. He adds the good news that it is just as accessible to us today through the spiritual practices of meditation, introspection, compassion, and unconditional love as it was when we were children."

—Michael Bernard Beckwith,

author of Life Visioning

Michael's Life Vision is so Brilliant!

"I was deeply touched by Temba's story. His simple reminiscence of his triumphs and his intense sense of the beauty of love produced soft tears clouding my vision as I read his manuscript. His undying respect for mothers despite his wounded childhood strengthened my faith in the Divine. As the mother of a child who was affected as he was, I have a special place for Temba in my heart. This book is a must read for anyone seeking to live a passionate life, as he is the greatest example of all."

—*Teri Shaughnessy, public speaker, entrepreneur, and author of* 101 Simple Truths for Creating a Passionate Life

Teri is so Focused & Creative

"A powerful and poignant message—deep and timely. In How to-**Reclaim Your Innocence**: _Remembering the Love-Beauty Within_, Temba Spirit shares the importance of honoring and loving ourselves as well as those around us every day. He captures the essence of our gentle spirits when we are born and the crucial need to continue to live in this type of love consistently. When we examine and share love, like Temba shows us how to do here, we actively create abundance for ourselves and those around us."

—**Shajen Joy Aziz**, M.Ed., Co-author of _Discover the Gift ~ It's Why We're Here_

Shajen is such an Adorable

Discovery & Gift

"Temba's words are like music to the ears. He effortlessly shares his story of overcoming and the journey to living a life of love or living from the heart. Temba's honest accounts show us that we can mobilize our lives with inner power, forgiveness and love. He lays the path out before us so that we can walk into the life of our choosing. Thank you Temba for writing such a powerful and pertinent text that can be help in bringing about healing for years to come."

—*Willetta Frizzle*, *Founder of* <u>*Frizzle Training*</u> <u>*and Consulting,*</u> *Life Coach and Trainer*

Willetta is on Fire & so Energized!

"Temba gives voice to every soul that has been victimized by life's circumstances, and truly models the courage to move beyond that victim consciousness into the true empowerment that can only come from a willingness to forgive. He inspires each of us to honor the bullet of mistrust lodged in our own heart and to build our own platform of compassion needed to find our way back to the child within us who holds our faith, hope, love, and trust."—***Cathryn Taylor****, MA, MFT, LADC, author of the bestselling Inner Child Workbook*

Cathryn is so Caring & Understanding

" When I look at Temba, hear him sing, learn his story, and read his words, I am profoundly humbled by the strength of the human spirit to prevail...always able to return to the purity of our hearts, as when we took our first breath."

—*Marcy Cole, Ph.D., Holistic Psychotherapist, Best Selling Co-Author, & Founder of "Childless Mothers Adopt" 501-c3*

Marcy is so Compassionate & Positive

"Temba Spirit reminds all of us in his deeply moving book, **How to-Reclaim Your Innocence:** _Remembering the Love-Beauty Within,_ that none of us exist in isolation – that each of us are intimately connected to one another, and that with that connection there is an unspoken responsibility to take our life's lessons, no matter how dark or how painful, and transform them into the gift that they are meant to be. Congratulations Temba! You have gone deep into the recesses of your own soul to remind us that we live in a benevolent universe. That everything is always working 'for us' not 'against us.' Through your transparency you have reminded us again that the greatest power in the universe lies within our own heart and when we decide to be the love that we are, anything is possible."

—_Janet Bray Attwood - New York Times Bestseller - Co/author of The Passion Test - The Effortless Path to Discovering Your Life Purpose_

Janet is so Passionate & Kind

"Ever since I was a little girl I thought, 'If only people could see the inside of another person, they would see their True Beauty & God Essence.' Temba Spirit's invitation to view humanity, individually and collectively, from their childlike innocence is a powerful & efficacious blueprint for creating Heaven on Earth!"

"Once in a great while, a book comes along that wakes us up and invites us to reach deeper into our hearts than we've ever journeyed. *How to Reclaim Your Innocence: Remembering the Love-Beauty Within is that book!"*

—*Dr. Elizabeth Lambaer* — *Inspirational Speaker, Talk Show Host & Author of Skinny Dipping in the Fountain of YOUTH... Seven Keys to Eternal Radiance!*

Elizabeth is so Radiant & Inspired!

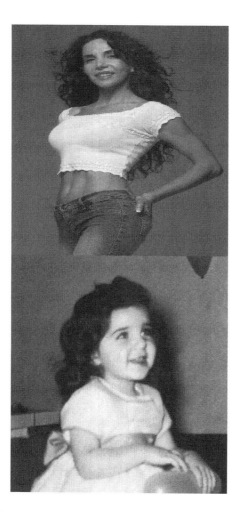

"Temba's story is truly inspirational and it touched me so deeply that my eyes welled up with tears. He reminds us that we are loved, that love is within us all and the innocence of who we are is the nature of the universe. Temba reminds us how truly precious we are and how important it is to honor and love yourself with all your heart. He has personally helped me rediscover the child in me and to embrace all that life has taught me. Living a life of passion, forgiveness, an open heart and having a giving nature is what it is truly all about. As Temba states in his book, 'You are loved by Love itself and that Love is within you, through you and all around you.' A simple Thank You Temba for reminding us all of this Love."

Poli—Freedom Life Coach, Mother. Founder of Freedom Coaching Australia.

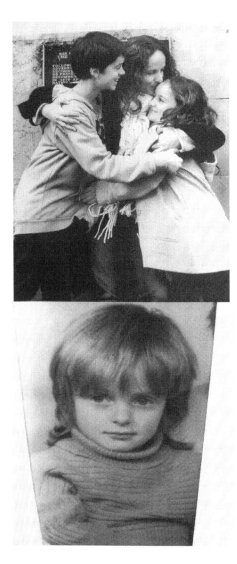

Poli is so

Open Heart-ed & Genuine

"When I read this book, I was reminded of my own birthright. I find myself looking in the mirror, as Temba suggests, and reminding myself that I arrived on the planet as Beloved. I still am, I always was! And thanks to Temba, I remember again the innocence of my babyhood, the joy of having an open, curious and playful heart. I am moved to live in this knowing, to carry this with me and share it with others."

—*Janice Christopher, Relationship Coach, Passion Test Facilitator, and host of "What's Ideal for You?" radio show www.WhatsIdealForYou.com*

Janice is so Beloved&Sweet

How to

Reclaim Your Innocence

Remembering the Love-Beauty Within

Temba Spirit

My Dedication

"I have gratefully learned how to transform the crap of my life into spiritual fertilizer! To this day, I am so fortunately blessed to live with a bullet that is still lodged in my chest. I now call this bullet "a bullet of Love." Though it almost killed me, it also was a great contributor in giving me the opportunity to embrace the most awesome power of forgiveness. For Somehow, someway, I walked up to the person who shot me, looked him in the eyes, and told him 'I forgive you.' Both fear and courage were present; however in that moment I chose to embrace the courage and Reclaim My Power! We all have this infinitely expansive capacity within us. I am not any more spiritual or

enlightened than anyone else. The great and awesome power to Love simply for the sake of Love is deeply woven into the fabric of each one of our hearts; I am absolutely convinced of this.

If I could forgive the person who tried to kill me, anyone can forgive their offender. I will always believe in the transcendent nature of the human heart. I therefore dedicate this book to the person who shot me and the bullet that almost killed me. The person who shot me gave me the gift of forgiving and even while in the midst of much pain, the opportunity to experience true Love. The bullet that barely missed my heart brought me closer to the very Love that is within my heart and this same perfect Love I know is within us all.

Life has taught me so much through suffering and tragedy. The most important lesson has been that no circumstance in the external world can destroy or taint in any way the essence of goodness that pervades everything. And that, of course, includes us. I now use my life's experiences to inspire, motivate, encourage, uplift, and nurture the heart of humanity. I love what my life has become. The greatest gift life has given me is to be able to Love and to serve."

I adore you so much.

Love, Temba Spirit

CONTENTS

ACKNOWLEDGEMENTS

To all the beloved hearts that responded when my heart called out for help

Thank You So Much..........

The way this book came together is a testimony of what it represents— which is **the irresistible and infinite power of Innocence and the infinite beauty of opened hearts that are aligned with the Supreme and Eternal principle of Love.** From the moment I began writing this book, the response of Divine Love has been swift and powerful! – Like the way that I spontaneously found my editor *Lynn Hess.*

"I believe there are no accidents in this beautiful life, and when Temba and I connected serendipitously and talked about his ideas for this book I immediately knew I wanted to be involved. Temba shines such a bright light, and I wanted to help bring it to the world. Throughout the editing process, our conversations started out with 'editing talk' but always ended up deepening into the philosophical and spiritual—and I was always amazed by the unique way in which the divine expresses itself through Temba's words. His boundless enthusiasm, radiant energy, and passionate desire to ease the suffering of others make him someone I'm proud to call a friend. It has been a privilege helping Temba share his message."

—*Lynn Hess*, *Chief Editor of* **How to Reclaim Your Innocence**: *Remembering the Love-Beauty Within*

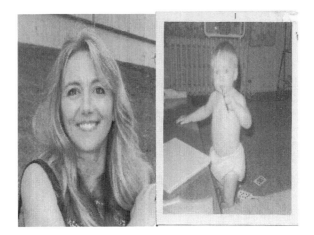

Lynn Hess is so Awesome & Precise!

Acknowledgments cont.

The parent of an *Innocent Heart* is Love and during the process of this book's formation, it has amazed and humbled me that there has not been one person that I asked for assistance that did not help me in the same way a concerned and Loving parent helps their very own beloved child. The ever-abundance and supreme energy of grace that moves through the human heart can even overwhelm me at times. Even now as I am writing this, the tears of gratitude are welling up within me. Each one of the people that have helped me represents one of my tear drops of gratitude. Their gracious support has revealed to me once again that Love is compelled to respond to the call of a selfless and innocent heart and that the simple yet profound eternal principles spoken of in this book — truly do work. There dwelling deep within the sacred heart of each one of my tears of gratitude is the longing and Innocent Desire for all beings to be free.

To all my beloved loved ones and friends who supported my heart's vision to write this book.

Thank you so much, Lynn Hess, Marci Shimoff, Debra Poneman, Janet Bray Atwood, Chris Atwood, Michael Bernard Beckwith, Rodney Scott, Marcy Cole, Beloved John Forrester, Anita Rehker, Dr. Elizabeth, Cathryn Taylor, Catherine Josey, Stacie Ratliff, My beloved Baba, MJ & Her son Paul, Liz Ramirez, Sonia Yanez, Denise Lambi, Poli, Kristi Stone, Grandma, Grandmamma, Mom, Leti Martinez, Tamara Perkins, Willetta Frizzle, All My homies that still live in me and also that are incarcerated, Shajen Aziz, Teri, Kenny" Knotie

Carter, Ian S. Blake, Kurt Hansen, Stacie Ratliff, Derick D-noc Stewart, Amma's beloved Devotees-Misha, My beloved Namrata, Somya Ma, Tripta, Jaya Krishnan, Eva Hoffmann, Sarah Uma Kane, Queen Ra, Para Bolten, Egyirba High, Dana Vaishnavi Fantuzzi, Julie (Tizzle) Jewels, Amulya and of course my beloved Spiritual Master Teacher and Universal Mother of Compassion—Amma.

International Baby Picture Day

To everyone who shared their baby pictures and collectively launched the Vision of *International Baby Picture Day*...Thank you so much. **May this begin a new era in which we collectively and brilliantly acknowledge, embrace, invoke and celebrate the innate Innocence, Beauty and Love- essence that is within all beings...............**

Love, Temba Spirit

Introduction

Who Is Temba Spirit?

I am exceedingly fortunate and super-abundantly grateful to be alive. I never thought for one minute when I was lying in the hospital bed, barely conscious with a bullet lodged in my chest, or even as a kid growing up in the impoverished community of Chicago's West Side, that this once broken, wretched and pitiful life would one day be used by the inexhaustible energy of Love to inspire, uplift and encourage absolutely anyone.

As a child, when my mom would repeatedly call me a bitch and tell me that she wished she would have flushed me down a toilet, how could I have known that through the vehicle of that very heartbreak and pain, my Spiritual Self and

Universal Child would one day be awakened and I would also become intimately acquainted with the Maternal and Eternal aspects, characteristics and principles of God? And when I was 12 years old and my beloved mom would have me buy weed for her, smoke a joint with me, and then kick me out so that she could entertain her boyfriend, I did not consider that this womb and pain would one day be used by Love to birth a new me.

I never imagined while homeless, lost, wretched, lonely, and spiritually bankrupt, sleeping on an old dirty recliner chair in a filthy hallway that I— who was so resentful of my mom — would be chosen by Love to one day honor and develop a deep heartfelt adoration for all mothers. Who would have thought that I, Temba Spirit, a former gang member and ex-convict considered by society to be useless and hopeless would, after all the bullshit and insanity, be sought out and end up touring the U.S. with Janet Bray Attwood and Chris Attwood, the New York Times bestselling book authors of *The Passion Test: The Effortless Path to Discovering Your Life Purpose?* I mean seriously, bestselling book authors and Life Purpose! Years ago, I would have probably robbed them if I saw them in my neighborhood. Nope, I never saw this coming! The only purpose I believed that I had at one point in my life was to sell and use drugs, rob and steal from people that cared about me and be a total let down for all those people who loved and believed in me. But lo! Through the all-wise supreme goodness of a universe that is always for us and never against us, at birth I was given the sacred and ancient name ***Temba*** which means — ***to give hope to the hopeless*** — and through the eternal vibration contained in that name, the purpose of my Life would benevolently unfold on its own accord.

Temba, you may ask, why did bestselling authors seek you out in the first place?

Good question! Janet heard about the *spiritual transformation* and experiences that occurred while I was incarcerated, and the humanitarian projects that I had initiated after I was released. She thought that I would be a complement to them in forming their empowerment program—a program that would help the homeless and young people in lock-down detention centers to discover their passions. This was right up my alley! My heart was hoping to find some people in the transformation world that were not afraid to come down to *"the hood."*

I used to ask people, **"How can the ancient truths reach all people if everything has a price tag on**

it? Should spiritual truth and healing practices not be as free as the air we breathe and available to everyone? If Love is universal, should it not be shared with all people regardless of their economic status?" I loved the universal message that I heard being conveyed in the self-help world but a lot of the packaging seemed very commercial and inauthentic. And to be honest with you, I had also experienced much racism and also was stereo-typed when I attended functions at different yoga and spiritual circles. I always knew that the ill-behaviors displayed by the followers of certain spiritual masters had nothing to do with their message of universal Love. **And anyway, how could I ever judge anyone knowing how unfairly I had treated many people in the past?**

Because of all I just mentioned above, anyone who was willing to come to the *"hood"* to share their heartfelt message and their love really touched me. So many people had been murdered around me when I was just a kid. If only someone had taken the time to help these people to discover the reason they were born in the first place. **If only someone would have looked beyond the stereotypes and the misinformed judgments and looked down into their souls, they would have seen Temba (Hope). They would have seen Spirit (Love).** And so many lives could have been saved. So many lives that were written off as meaningless would have been discovered to have had divine significance. This realization pained me intensely but it also moved me into action and helped me to heal. For at some point I realized that death was a myth and that none of them had really died. Instead they all still lived forever strong within the precious and sacred heart of humanity and also within the collective eternal memory of a universally conscious and omnipresent and perfect Love. It would, therefore, be through my Life and yours that their lives would inherit everlasting meaning.

The Journey Continues

So here I was, hanging out with bestselling authors. They had something to share with me and I had something to share with them, but what? You know, in Life there is always more there than what meets the eye. In a short period of time, Janet, Chris, and I really connected deeply in the heart. I was quickly catapulted into a world filled with more bestselling book authors, transformational personalities, spiritual leaders, celebrities and a host of many other beautiful people from all walks of life.

And get this! Somehow I ended up on the same stage as a special guest performer with Byron Katie (*Loving What Is, The Work*), Mark Victor Hansen and Jack Canfield (*Chicken Soup for the Soul)* and Michael Bernard Beckwith and Rickie Byars Beckwith (*Agape International Spiritual Center, The Secret*). I was even interviewed by Marci Shimoff, a woman who has sold over fourteen million self-help books.

Even during my days of getting into a lot of trouble, my aunt and others used to tell me that I had a good heart, but I never took it too seriously. Deep down I have always cared for people. I never saw it as anything special and I still don't. But I tell you, you never know how you are affecting people.

"Temba has been a great inspiration to me, as he is a wonderful role model of service and love towards others. In fact, I respect Temba so much that I

interviewed him for my upcoming book 'Love for No Reason.' He is one of the 150 'Love Luminaries' I interviewed about unconditional love (along with top scientists, psychologists, subject matter experts, and spiritual teachers) and Temba's was one of the most wise, profound, and moving of all the interviews."

—Marci Shimoff, #1 NY Times bestselling author of—Love for No Reason and Happy for No Reason

What a great honor it was for Debra Poneman (*Chicken Soup for the American Idol Soul*) to invite me to be a guest speaker at her renowned "Yes to Success" seminar. Debra is considered to be one of the pioneers of the transformational movement and a mentor of Marci Shimoff, Janet Attwood, and numerous other transformational leaders. Even more important than that, Debra is my dear friend. In fact Debra, Janet, and Marci are all cherished by me. I consider them to be the three big sisters that I never had. Their Love has stuck by me through thick and thin.

"Temba is the real deal. He doesn't just talk about love, he embodies it. When my 21-year-old son—a young man who joined our family when he was 15—was in jail, as soon as I told Temba what had happened, he

immediately went down to 26th and California to visit him so that Ke'juan would know that there were people who were pulling for him. Temba had never even met Ke'juan before—and he didn't do it to get praise or points. He did it because he grabs every opportunity he can to give love just because that's who he is.

The other night someone gave us tickets to a show in downtown Chicago and as we walked along the streets and stood in line, Temba's saying hi and talking to everyone in the crowd. He's just connecting with the people and I'm watching them transform and open up in front of my eyes because of Temba's love. And he is an equal-opportunity love-giver...white, black, male, female, old, young, homeless, million-aire...it doesn't matter to Temba. If you happen into his space, you're fair game for his love, compassion, and generosity of spirit. I mean, who does that—besides Temba?! This man is a true gift to the planet."

—Debra Poneman, founder and president Yes to Success, Inc., bestselling author of—Chicken Soup for the American Idol Soul

You may be wondering, "How did this guy do it?" "What is his secret?" "Did he *steal* their hearts?" Yep! That's exactly what I did! **As a convicted felon I stole things that did not belong to me. As a servant of humanity— like a thief in the night—I steal hearts that all belong to Love.**

As all of this interacting, connecting of hearts, and touring was occurring, I, who had come from a very different background, (or so it seemed on the surface) often pondered, "How did I get here?" After all, I had never visualized, intentioned, affirmed, consciously applied any techniques, or even once thought about hanging out with transformational celebrities. And in all realness, there were times when I just did not feel worthy. The mind can be such a strange and silly foe but the heart is all-powerful and its super-abundant strength helped me to get over that silly *mind stuff* very quickly. Through allowing my heart to dictate my reality—I became very aware that I was there for a reason—and that reason was to realize that it was not about me. **We are all here not by accident or mistake. Life's beloved and benevolent purpose is indeed for us to be here. How do we know this? Because we are here! Yet at the same time it is not about us.** I gratefully realized early on that it was not about me as much as it was about what would and could happen through me. This is the divine paradox and beauty of Life Purpose.

This is clearly what it was and is about: **For years my heart had longed intensely, hoping that the best the transformational and healing world had to offer would be shared with those of less fortunate circumstances. Those who had suffered on the streets as I had—the homeless, the addicts, the suicidal, the downtrodden, the judged, the rejected, the orphans, the lonely, the lost, the** abandoned, the widows, the hopeless, the incarcerated, the forgotten. I had unknowingly tapped into the innate universal qualities of innocence and compassion that we all have deep within. In forgetting me, I became free.

The Breast Milk of Your Love

There have been many days and nights in which I have shed tears of compassion on behalf of the forgotten, hoping to invoke a response from the very heart of humanity—similar to the way babies cry when they are hungry, hoping to be fed by their mother's breast milk. When a baby cries like this, the mother's breasts are spontaneously filled with milk to the point that it may even pain her. **When we feel the hunger of a hurting humanity longing for our love, our hearts are filled with love in this same way.** We *all* therefore have the capacity to breastfeed all innocent life with our spiritual breast milk of love. This is a universal and natural law.

My heart has always been hungry for humanity's love and it still is. I have suffered so much and I did not want anyone to suffer as I had. My heart broke into pieces when it realized that there were millions that suffered far worse than I. I longed for their lives to be saturated with my, yours, ours, anyone's Love and I still do. My Love will never forget the forgotten and neither will yours. We are one in love and there is really just one heart. This one beloved heart, this one beloved friend of friends, emanates its infinite energy of compassion through each and every one of us in its own unique and beautiful way. In this my faith is unshakable!

Beloved Little Ricky

This reminds me of one of my most treasured experiences. When I was just a child, my best friend Little Ricky's family was much poorer than mine. One Christmas I literally received every toy that I had asked for. Little Ricky received none. On Christmas Day he came over to play with all of my toys. I noticed how much joy he had as he played with the toys. I also knew that when he left, that he would have none to play with at home. This made me sad and broke my heart into pieces of compassion. The next day, when Little Ricky came by to play with me, I gave him each and every one of my favorite toys! That is what I chose to do with the broken pieces of my heart. It made me feel so good to know that this would make him happy.

Never once did I ever think about asking for my toys back. Growing up, my heart would overflow with joy every time I thought about my decision and it still does to this day. **The next time your heart breaks into pieces of compassion as it notices someone in need, offer those broken pieces in innocence and help them. Those very broken pieces will then be used to mend the broken heart of humanity.** I did not know it then, but I now understand that I had spontaneously experienced bliss and had been given a huge glimpse and taste of selfless love.

Every good thing that my heart has wanted for others has always come to me. It sometimes feels selfish to live a life of selfless intention. I always get my way. I have learned through personal experience that Love is compelled to respond to a selfless call. **When life offers its benevolent gifts to us, we remain free and**

overflowing with Love by offering the gifts life has given us to others. The way we keep love is by sharing love. Love has an infinite supply of itself, so in giving it away you will never run out. Life then becomes a great ever-expanding *circle of Love and compassion* and as simple and effortless as breathing.

I learned through direct experience that the secret to opening the door of the universal heart is to want others to have the best life has to offer, even more than we want it for ourselves. You see, the longing to want love to be experienced by others is the best that life and love have to offer. That longing indeed is our love wanting to be in union with every heart and all life. When our hearts respond to life in this way, the longing takes us into the realm of oneness, connectedness, and union. **This is the yoga of the heart.**

Once we become aware that we are an important part of the whole, the *all goodness that is always present effortlessly comes to us* and also becomes our ongoing and natural experience. **Once you taste true Love, you just want that spiritual food to be shared with everyone. You realize that on the plate of Love there is an infinite supply and more than enough for absolutely everyone to eat.** We just have to learn to care, and then in that caring begin to share out of the abundance of our very own heart.

The Spiritual Solution Is So Simple

Here is a good example of how the simplicity and beauty of Love can work collectively. Let's say there are 11 people sitting around the dinner table. Ten of the people have full plates, and one person has an empty plate. One of the people who have a full plate makes a great suggestion: "Let's all share one nice heaping spoonful from each of our plates with the person whose plate is empty." They all agree. The empty plate is passed around the dinner table and returns full and barely has room for another bit of food. **The 10 people look at their plates and smile because not only are their plates still full, but they have shared what they had with someone who had nothing.** Feeding someone who had nothing became much more important to them than eating more than they needed. Their hearts are full and now brimming over with Love, and the person who had nothing has a full stomach.

This, beloved, is the path to bliss, innocence, compassion, simplicity, and true love. It's not something reserved only for the spiritual elite, it is something that can be experienced by anyone who breathes. **There is no greater gift than to love** so deeply that you forget yourself and become lost in that very love.

I base my entire spiritual life around what I learned through my experiences with my beloved best friend Little Ricky. I value those experiences even more today—for sadly, Little Ricky ended up being one of my many childhood friends that was brutally murdered. But lo! Little Ricky still lives! In my heart and now in yours as well! **Life is such a precious gift; please do all you can to treasure each moment of this beloved and blessed journey.**

Now Let's Continue the journey...

So here I was, an ex-gang member and ex-convict who people now wanted to be around! It was the Love-energy emanating through and from my heart that was the attractive element; I now know this. The labels the world gives you are irrelevant once you leave the road the world has laid forth and begin your sacred journey on the path of spiritual bliss. Society's negative labels are not welcomed there.

The Infinite Value of the Heart

Not only did people want to be around me, they also greatly valued the spiritual gifts that I had to share and I also greatly valued theirs. **Many of them were economically prosperous, but I saw them as human beings first. When I spoke to them, I did not speak to the wealth of their money, I spoke to the wealth of their hearts. I believe they really appreciated this.**

Of all the spiritual experiences that I have ever had, there has been none greater than connecting in the heart with another human being. I discovered that my gift, my purpose, and my passion were not to be found in the details, but in the essence/heart. My number one passion would simply be to adore Life and to serve Life. **I would make my permanent home humanity's heart. I would therefore never have to be homeless again. My life's purpose would become my very breath of life. Remembering to love in each moment would become my spiritual practice. Simplicity would become my path to reclaiming my power!**

As I have already stated, I began noticing that my heart's wanting for others to have the best was attracting that same best reality to me. One of the ways this universal law profoundly and boldly showed up in my life was being embraced by Janet and Chris. They gave me their best!

During one of my performances I looked out at the audience and noticed tears streaming down Chris's face. I asked him after the perform- mance why he was crying. He looked at me with watery eyes and said, "Temba, I know you have been through so much." The source of his tears emerged from his heart of compassion, the same place that mine and everyone else's comes from.

And, speaking of compassion:

What Would I Do Without AMMA?

Initially, as I said, Janet and Chris just wanted me to help design a curriculum for their book that would specifically support people in prisons and homeless shelters to discover their passions. Janet had heard about the humanitarian work that I was doing through the support, guidance, and inspiration of my Spiritual Master *Amma*, the world-renowned humanitarian and hugging saint from India. One of the programs I initiated through the inspiration and backing of Amma is **"Circle of Love Inside,"** a letter-writing and outreach program that began behind the walls of prison. And thanks to the dedication of many beautiful-hearted people, this program is now in every major city in the U.S. and also in India.

It was my spiritual teacher Amma who first embraced me while I was incarcerated via my dreams, and also my remembrance of how she herself had suffered tremendously as a child but had overcome it all through exercising the principles of Love, forgiveness, and compassion. To know that a being of that magnitude understood my pain helped me to hold on during many rough times and also helped me to awaken. Like myself, Amma had also been abused as a child and had been misunderstood by the world and considered an outcast of her society. She even experienced great prejudice because of her dark black skin. **As far as I was concerned, Amma wasn't just my spiritual teacher, she was one of**

my homies (dearly loved friends) I had grown up with. I had come from the hood of Chicago and Amma had come from the hood of Kerala, India. To me, Amma was one of us, yet I knew that the picture and reality of Amma was much bigger than that.

When Amma embraced me, I was literally smothered by the awareness of unconditional love. At the time I felt very wretched and unworthy; however, when I remembered the unconditional Love that the universal Mother had for all beings, in that moment that quality re-awakened in me. **Though I was surrounded by society's so-called useless, horrendous, and wretched, once the universal Mother came alive within me, I knew then that there was no life that Divine Love could not recycle and transform into pure gold.** I contemplated deep within my heart, *"If Love loves me— this Love also loves everyone!"*

I contemplated again, **"I am not any more special than anyone else. We are all just as special to Love. These men have to know how loved they are and they will know this through Amma working through my very own heart. Amma has awakened the Love within my heart and as Her son, I will awaken the Love within the men."** I had gone crazy! For months I wrapped my white prison bed sheet around me and like a mad man and I pretended that I was the Divine Mother, who always wears a white sari.

My time while incarcerated would be dedicated to leading people to the Love within their very own beings. I felt that I had been given so much and I had no choice but to share what had been so freely shared with me. It did not matter what their religion or way of Life was—my message was universal Love. In one of Amma's books I had read that Amma feeds all of Her children before She Herself eats and many times She doesn't even eat. This idea moved me profoundly! I began purchasing food from the prison store so that I could feed the entire prison dorm. I made sure I offered my food and my heart to anyone around me that seemed depressed or alone. **I wanted to be just like Amma.** Her Love had placed a pull on my heart that I could not resist. I had fallen deeply in Love with the universal principles of motherhood. I willingly and enthusiastically studied as many religions as I could in hopes that it would help me create a bridge to connect more deeply with the men— **who to me were no longer convicts. To the experience of my heart they had become Amma's darling and beloved children— which meant that they had become my children and I theirs. Many of the men thought I was crazy but as time carried on they all came to Love me.**

This reminds me of something Amma once said, "Anyone—man or woman—who has the courage to overcome the limits of the mind, can obtain the state of universal motherhood. The love of awakened motherhood is a loving compassion not only for one's own children but for all people, animals, plants, rocks, rivers. It is a love extended to all nature's beings. For one who has awakened to true motherhood, every creature is his or her child. Such love, such motherhood, is divine Love, which is God." —Amma

I do not claim to have attained that permanent state of being. All my heart knew and still knows is that it wants to be just like *Amma*— just like unconditional Love—just like uncompromising compassion and just like **your heart**. I looked for the men who were in the deepest pain, hoping to console, comfort, and embrace them. I would tell them, **"You are loved**

by Love itself and that Love is within you, through you and all around you." With all of my heart's strength, I would continue by telling them that there was absolutely nothing they could do to change that. Just in telling them this, the tears of Love would effortlessly emerge and spontaneously pour through them. In that openness and raw space of the heart, **I would embrace them and feel their teardrops fall on my shoulders. These men were my saviors and they were healing me. In my heartfelt desire for them to experience true Love, they had given me a reason to live.**

Each day when I awoke, my number one purpose and resolve was to invoke the tears of Love within someone's heart. When this happened, I knew that I had helped them to tap the God-Consciousness within. This is what Amma and all the Masters had taught me. They all taught me to discover, experience, and reveal the universal Love that not only was within my heart but was my heart.

With the beloved Christians, I prayed in the name of the Lord and Savior Jesus Christ. Christianity became important to me because it was important to them. When I hung out with the Muslims, I prayed in the illustrious and beneficent name of Allah and greeted them by saying "Salaam Alaykum." Islam became important to me because it was important to them. With those who wanted to, I chanted Om Namah Shivaya. With the Native Americans, I sang ancient ceremonial songs, sweat in the Sacred Lodges, and prayed to The Great Spirit/Wakan Tanka. There was even an Ethiopian Jew, and African Hebrew Israelites who I would read the Torah with and would greet by saying "Shalom." **Whatever was important to them became important to me!**

You would be amazed to discover that there are thousands of light beings behind prison walls that have been placed there to preserve the legacy of spiritual culture and to help others awaken. *

The Spiritual Masters

So it is mainly the Spiritual Masters of the East that have taught me how to experience Life as a Universal being—and the one particular Master that I have fallen deeply in Love with is Amma! And how could I not have, considering all I just told you? Could little ol' Temba Spirit resist the unconditional and omnipotent Love of the Divine Mother who is teaching me to see Life and everything in it as God? Because I know the universal Mother forever adores me, that contemplation compels my heart to adore you.

Had it not been for Amma I probably would have given up on myself. Not only did she lead me to the love within my very own heart, she shined a light on me in a way that attracted the attention of so many other wonderful human beings in the transformational community. Some call this the Grace of the Guru. **We all need someone to embrace our good, even when it appears that there is very little present or none there at all. Amma was that person for me. She helped me to notice my very own innate Innocence, Beauty, Love, and Goodness.**

It would be nice to say that I taught all of this to myself and just magically became aware of whom and what I really am, but that would be very inauthentic and unreal. During my days of intense suffering, I have always had a spiritual teacher appear to me to give me guidance when I most needed it. I have also had various experiences that have revealed to me that the internal and external teacher are one—and this is the great lesson that many people on the spiritual path miss.

As a spiritual guide, Amma has opened up doors to my success that will never close. The greatest door that she opened was the one to my heart—and how she did this was by simply believing in me when I most needed someone to. **As long as our hearts remain open, the doorway to our success remains open. Whatever helps our hearts to open should be celebrated and adored.**

I therefore adore Amma just as I adore my very own heart. Jesus, Buddha, Allah, Yahweh, Wakan Tanka, Amma, my heart, your heart, and the heart of all—become the same thing when you embrace them all as the source of Love and the essence of All Life. **A true teacher will lead you to the essence of your very own being and give** you the tools to expand in that awareness. Life itself is the true teacher.

I once asked Amma to bless my life to bring those who had suffered like me to the arms of her love. Amma responded, **"Your innocent desire will happen in time."** After that, I brought droves of homeless people, inner city kids, gang members, and many others to meet Amma. I also noticed that Amma said, **"Your innocent desire."** I had no choice but to realize that this God-Conscious desire had emerged out of the depths of me! Yet I remained aware that the quality of Innocence was universal and had its source in everyone. This great and expansive power of innocent desire moved me profoundly. I began bringing former prostitutes from the city on camping trips and into nature. I have always felt that we all deserve to experience the beauty of breathing clean air. I named the service "Innocent Desire" after the words that Amma had spoken to me.

This innocent desire was so intense and concentrated that it moved me to spontaneously start a project that went on to build a house for an orphan family in the poorest area in the country! I used to tell people, **"If Amma can build over 25,000 homes in India, why can't I at least build one here in America?"** That is the power and resolve of a living spiritual master, which as I stated, is no different from the power that emanates in and through our very own hearts. You've got to catch this! **You cannot genuinely acknowledge what you do not have yourself. Everything you study while on the spiritual path whether it is on the inside of you, or the outside of you, is a study of yourself.**

Adoring the one that blesses our success

Also know this, beloved: All of the self-help book authors and transformational personalities that I know of also had spiritual teachers who opened up doors for them and blessed their success. For example, Janet, Chris, Marci, and Debra's guru was **Maharishi Mahesh Yogi**—the same teacher the Beatles followed. I want to personally say **JAI GURU DEV** to the great Master Maharishi Mahesh Yogi and to the community of Fairfield, Iowa for all the tremendous support over the years. I jokingly tell people that I made it there before **Oprah.**

The bottom line is.......

The modern day self-help and transformational movement would not have manifested in the profound way that it has, had it not been for the Great Masters such as

Paramahansa Yogananda, Baba Muktananda, Swami Satchinanda, Swami Vivekananda and many other Saints who came from the East to help the beings in the West to awaken. Even **Martin Luther King Jr.**, one of humanity's greatest modern day spiritual leaders, was, according to his own writings, greatly influenced by **Mahatma Gandhi**. And Gandhi himself said in his own writings that he was influenced by the great Master of Compassion—**Jesus the Messiah**.

Though I now realize that the external teacher and the internal teacher are one, I will still always have a special appreciation and eternal adoration for Amma—**for when society labeled me an outcast, She called me her darling son Temba.**

A few kind words...

*"When I first heard about Temba,
I found out that he had started a
letter-writing campaign for
inmates at Rikers Island so they
would know someone cared. This
year, Temba created a program
to empower and support a Native
American orphan family in the
poorest area in the country, the
Pine Ridge reservation in South
Dakota. Not only did he attract
financial support, he also
inspired college students and
others to assist him in teaching
the local natives how to build
their own natural homes and
grow their own food. Temba did*

41

this while in the midst of his music career starting to take off.

Temba chose, instead of music, money, and fame, to make sure that those less fortunate had adequate housing, heat, clothes, and food. I love this man. We have spent many hours traveling together to help others in need. During that time I was fortunate to get to know him deeply. He is a very giving and kind man."

—Janet Attwood, *New York Times bestselling author of —The Passion Test: The Effortless Path to Discovering Your Life Purpose*

Reclaim Your Power!

When Janet and Chris invited me to my first *Passion Test* facilitator seminar to help them design the program, little did they know that I was not just a humanitarian but also a performing artist! They allowed me to do my rap song, *Power Thoughts* —"**These words that I speak to the air, Power Thoughts. Perfect sight my vision is clear, Power Thoughts. In Perfect Love there's nothing to fear, Power Thoughts!**" Everyone loved it! Janet and I had both jumped way out of our boxes and comfort zones. Hip-hop meets the self-help movement—isn't that a trip? And it worked! We broke the mold and the new paradigm had begun!

After that, they asked me to write *The Passion Test* theme song! Everything happened so fast and it was all spontaneous and effortless. A couple of weeks later, I received a call from Janet: "Temba, I need you to write a song called **Reclaim Your Power!**" I, of course, said yes! I called her back in a couple of minutes and asked, "Janet what exactly do you mean by *Reclaim Your Power?*" She replied,**"You know, when you were young you had a dream and a vision and you saw life through the eyes of love, and you let it go. I want you to write a song about reclaiming that!"** I very easily fell in love with the concept of the song. Who could not relate to that?

I innocently placed my favorite picture of *Amma* on the kitchen counter top and, as if glued to that spot, I wrote the song in a few days. The song took the transformational world by storm, and I performed it before thousands! I performed it while touring with Amma and also at a gathering for **President Obama** in Beverly Hills hosted by **Louis Gossett, Jr.**

It wasn't until later that Janet revealed to me that the title **Reclaim Your Power** had emerged out of a conversation between her and her dear friend **Michael Bernard Beckwith, founder and Spiritual Director of Agape International Spiritual Center.** On the same day that Janet called me, she had also asked Michael, **"What do I say when I go talk to people in homeless shelters and to the kids in lock-down detention centers?"** Michael had replied, **"Janet, tell them that it's time to reclaim their power!"**

I had no idea that this conversation between Michael and Janet had occurred until months after touring the U.S. I went on to perform **Reclaim Your Power!** in front of an audience of thousands at Michael Bernard Beckwith's and Rickie Beckwith's Spiritual Center in L.A. The other act on the bill was **Deva Premal** and **Mitten**. Can you imagine, Conscious Hip-hop and ancient

Sanskrit chanting all being stirred up in one universal pot of love? Now that's a new paradigm! The Agape International Spiritual Center's stage was set on fire that day—and so were so many hearts. It was a great joy to serve and I probably was the greatest spiritual benefactor, for I have learned through personal spiritual experience that the reward of service is to continually be able to serve!

A few months later I was invited by incredibly talented Rickie Beckwith to be a special guest at Agape's annual spiritual extravaganza, *"Revelations."* Months after that, I had Rickie as my special guest performer at my second *Circle of Compassion* benefit concert.

"Temba has attended many services with my congregation, Agape International Spiritual Center in Los Angeles, California, as well as performing his song "Reclaim Your Power" before my congregation of 10,000. But our friendship goes beyond the walls of my community. I have known him for five years, and am very familiar with his selfless work with Native Americans, those incarcerated, and the homeless community. Temba's commitment to peace and to genuine compassion and caring are among his finest qualities."

—**Michael Bernard Beckwith**

Consciousness Is Truly Universal

So, beloved friends, both the energy and intention in this book are packed with a rich spiritual legacy and an unstoppable conscious resolve! That simply means that I poured my whole heart into it—just as so many beautiful-hearted people poured their hearts into me. I bow to the Divine Love within them all. The pouring out of this breast milk of Love will not stop! Just imagine thousands of people chanting in unison, "It's time to reclaim your power!" The more I perform the song, the more I realize that the title **Reclaim Your Power** is universal and can be applied to anyone who is open. Children, teenagers, adults, and elders of every persuasion are always inspired. When I sign autographs, many people approach me in tears.

I have also noticed that many people in the universally conscious community are misinformed about "rap music." Like many others, they have it wrapped up in the boxes of stereotypes and believe that Hip-hop music is limited to the unhealthy stuff you hear on mainstream radio. After they hear my song **Reclaim Your Power** and the many other love-inspired Hip-hop songs, something within them shifts! Many people approach me and say things like, "You really helped me. I didn't know Rap music could be that inspiring and powerful!" I playfully ask, "Can you quote one lyric from any rap song?" Most people cannot. I then just smile and give them a hug. Because **Reclaim Your Power** is endorsed by well-known transformational personalities and is packed with nothing but Love energy, it helps people transcend their stereotypes and judgments (egos).

To help people relax, I sometimes say, **"God was the first Hip-hop lyricist!** In the beginning was the Word (lyric)!"

The Book

I know I am not the only one who has had challenges in life and has a story. **Each and every one of our lives is a sacred scripture.** I feel honored and humbled that you have allowed me to share a little of my scripture/story with you. In this crazy world of emotional let down, financial crisis, materialism, confusion, natural catastrophe, and spiritual bankruptcy, who doesn't need to reclaim his or her power? And what is true spiritual power really? Is not true spiritual power to be found in the sacred qualities of the heart?

When we were children, each and every one of us saw life through the eyes of Love, Innocence, and Beauty, or, simply put, the heart. When we were children we embodied the Law of Attraction. This was not just one of us, this was all of us! We were the center of attention because Love is the center of all attention. And here is the great news, beloved friend. Through remembering, simplicity, openness, and consistent practice, each and every one of us can reclaim the innate innocence, beauty, and love that we were as children and that we all are even **Now.** You see, in a moment's time, you can reclaim your innocence and once again be aligned with the support of the entire universe! Through all my hardships and overcoming this is the great lesson that life has taught me. I will always be someone's beloved child. That someone is Love. With all of my heart I invite you into this world.

So, when I looked up and was literally surrounded by a number of bestselling book authors who all loved me and wanted to see me succeed, my inner voice said, "Duh, write a book!" I had always been told that I was a good writer and this was also a way in which I could give a little back to the stream of life as it has so freely and willingly given me. If I could write powerful songs, why not powerful books as well? Well, beloved friends, here it is: *How to-__Reclaim Your__ __Innocence:__ __Remembering__ the __Love-Beauty__ __Within__*

What I share with you is not my belief, nor my philosophy; **it is my direct experience as a potential Master who is yet still in training.** We are all Masters in training, ever-unfolding in the all-goodness of a beautiful and beloved Life. I sincerely hope that you enjoy this offering of compassion and that it helps you to fall in Love with your very own heart as you take this journey down this most sacred path of remembering and reclaiming who you really are.

I adore you so much. Love, Temba Spirit

Live at Agape International Spiritual Center

Manose, Temba Spirit, Michael Bernard Beckwith, Deva Premal, Mitten, Janet Bray Atwood and Chris Atwood

I will reveal much more of this in my book, The Compassion of a Convicted Felon: When a Prison Cell Becomes the Heart of God (Divine Love). Please stay tuned.

Temba Spirit holding 2 year old Cadance American Horse at the Pine Ridge reservation in South Dakota

Chapter 1

Innocence Is a Universal Quality That Belongs to All of us

> *"A child can attract anyone's attention; even the most cold-hearted person will have some good feelings towards a child. This attraction is due to the innocence of the child. When you are free from the grip of the ego, you, yourself, will become as innocent and playful as a child."*
>
> *—Amma*

When we were children, we experienced life through the eyes of wonder, innocence, beauty, and love. This is not some of us; this is the experience and reality of every child that is born into this world. Each and every last one of us— just as we are is—absolutely adorable. There is absolutely nothing in this world that can change that. Each and every one of us came here with the awareness of the Universal Child and the supreme consciousness of perfect Innocence.

Please consider for a few moments, that you, as well as every person that has ever offended or hurt you, has incarnated into this world as infinitely precious and also as perfect embodiments of absolute, inexhaustible and unconditional-Divine Love.

As children we lived life as if it was a dream, and because our very life was that adventurous dream, we had no need or desire to seek one. Even during times when we were hurt, like seasoned spiritual masters we effortlessly let go and moved into the next moment with perfect ease. We did not have to forgive when we were hurt by others. Our constant state was to see the benevolence and creative brilliance in everyone. **As children we were willing to give everyone the benefit of the doubt and offering a second chance to someone was effortless.** A child will even find the *essence of goodness* in someone who is abusing them. It is only later on in life when we begin *"thinking"* about how we have been wronged that we develop resentments and animosity towards our offenders. Children embody God-Consciousness. They do not complicate life like we adults do. Children simply flow with the universal harmony and the natural ryhthems and law's of life. They only need to be taught how to maintain this exalted state and also acquire the discrimination and wisdom to harness their innocence in the most effective way.

So many of us were not shown or taught how to maintain this inner world of spiritual wonder and blessed natural state of being. As we *"grew up"* we absorbed the world's confusion and its cold-heartedness. **Our physical bodies developed; however our super natural spiritual state of Innocence, Beauty and Love was covered over by life's pains, pleasures, and unhealthy belief systems and society's over- emphasis on adult responsibilities and technological advancements.** As adults we inherited a *spiritual amnesia* and forgot that we were precious, priceless and awesomely adorable. We lost the awareness of who we really are. We dropped from the state of experiencing pure consciousness as children to experiencing pure ego as adults.

As children we lived in a state of consciousness in which all good things were possible. We were priceless and precious and also infinitely adorable in the eyes of the entire world around us. We expressed and exposed ourselves fearlessly, with no apprehension and to the fullest. Being totally naked in front of the world was seen as the sweetest and cutest thing. Why? Because without even intellectually understanding what Innocence was we embodied it perfectly! **Am I not describing you, beloved and most precious child of Love?**

There was a time in your life that you ran around the house and backyard completely naked and it was seen by the world as the most adorable sight. There are many tribes and villages that have not been influenced by this world's nonsense and they exist in pristine nakedness simply because their tribal and collective consciousness has not lost its innocence. **They are still in the Garden of Eden (delight).** Civilization with its corrupt, twisted and manipulative influences have not caused them to fall from Grace. Children live in the Garden of Eden state of consciousness just as tribal people that have not been affected and infected by this world do. Because children have just arrived to this plane of existence fresh from the source and essence of Life, they have not yet inherited the strange and selfish ways of this world.

This is a picture of an un-contacted and uncontaminated family in the Amazon that has not lost their beloved Innocence. They will forever live in the Garden of Eden state of consciousness and eat from the sacred Tree of Life unless this world's nonsense comes along and offers them the tree of worldly knowledge, confusion, disharmony, ego and its strange selfish ways. Let's all collectively visualize a world in which this tribe and all Innocent Life everywhere is protected, respected and adored to the fullest. We can participate in this much needed preservation right inside of our own homes first starting with and within ourselves.

As children

No one taught us how to be children and embody these qualities. It was our natural state of being. The emanation of perfect Love and the fearless reflection of spiritual and physical nakedness is the universal expression of *all* children. When we were children we did not have a religion, a spiritual practice, a teacher, or a technique, nor did we have to read any self-help books or sacred scriptures. Our very nature was infinitely beautiful and we were the perfectly manifested Book of Life walking, running, singing, laughing, dancing and playing on this earth. We entered into this world as embodiments of innocence and spiritual brilliance and creative genius, yet even those words fall short in describing the glory and divine presence of the sacred child that you were then and **You are still, even now.**

Please embrace this with Your Whole Heart

I want you to take what I am saying to you personally. Embrace this with your entire being. Own it and take a moment to reflect on this deeply. This is who you were then and somewhere underneath all the layers of Life's pains and pleasures, it is who you still are even now. You are, even now, someone's beloved and most treasured and cherished child. That someone is Infinite Love. You are one of the offspring of Supreme Love. You are infinitely priceless and precious.

There is absolutely nothing you can do to change that. Neither ego, nor any one of our issues or doubts or failures – or successes for that matter – can alter this divine reality. **And though your accomplishments may appear to add to your divine splendor,** I have got news for you beloved friend. You are perfectly and brilliantly manifested just as you are with or without your accomplishments. **Please do not love and adore yourself only based upon your qualifications or your accomplishments. You are infinitely adorable just as you are.** Life itself in its infinite brilliance has already qualified you to be unexplainable and beyond ordinary comprehension. You are an unexplainable being and something to be marveled at. What mother loves their child only for what their child can do? A mother loves their children simply because that is her marvelous and wonderful nature. A mother always sees her beloved children as much more than the negative or even the positive labels that the world places on them. **If you only love yourself because of what you have accomplished, that is how you will love others. And thus the love in this world will remain as inauthentic and synthetic and as counterfeit as it has been.**

Without the distractions and taint of an adult intellect filled with a lot of worldly knowledge and things defined by a collective unconscious society, as children we saw life through the eyes of a heart that was filled with supreme bliss. We effortlessly loved our neighbors as we loved ourselves without even intellectually knowing what love was. It is with your opened and available heart and not your knowledge-filled worldly and adult intellect that your innocence can, will and must be reclaimed.

Your First Spiritual Teacher was YOU!

When we were children our imaginations were boundless and unlimited! We did not have to find our life purpose. There was no need to even think about it. As children we embodied purpose! Every breath that we breathed, tear that we shed, and fun that we had, and even the naughty behavior we displayed was the fulfillment of our life purpose and destiny. Life was spontaneous, and with our entire being we did not waste one second. Each and every one of us was once a precious little baby. Each and every one of us is still even now, a precious and sacred and little angelic baby. You will always be someone's little baby. Our bodies have grown, now we must grow and expand our innocence. **Innocence is a universal quality that we all have in common.** Are we not all precious and brilliantly manifested forms of Life even now?

Now all we have to do is stretch and exercise this awareness. We did not lose our innocence and preciousness. You cannot lose who you really are. **It is only who we really are not that can be lost.** We only have to regularly practice the sacred art form (heart-form) of remembering and reclaiming.

Everything we now read about in spiritual books hoping to become we already were as children.

Your first spiritual teacher was **YOU!** The first sage, saint, mystic, and transformational personality in your life was **YOU! All the spiritual attributes that you now strive to attain as an adult you embodied as a *child.* Please remember this. It is so important.** Contemplate this deep in your heart. I mean really contemplate this deeply with all the full energy of your heart and soul.

Your Beloved Baby Picture

Do you have any of your baby pictures, or maybe even video footage? If you do, look at them as frequently as possible and behold your innocence and beauty and brilliant form. Out of the formless and most sacred ever-expanding womb of cosmic consciousness you have emerged in sublime Beauty. Take your time and let the remembrance of your Innocence nurture you. **And if you absolutely do not have a baby picture of yourself, please feel free to look at anything that helps you invoke your innate qualities of goodness and that helps to nurture your expanded awareness.** When you do this with an opened heart, your worldly intellectual head knowledge will die in your heart's remembrance and re-emerge in true spiritual wisdom. **True spiritual wisdom is to know who you really are.**

Commit to looking at your baby and childhood pictures each and every day. This is a great spiritual practice. And know that any practice that opens your heart and keeps it open is a great spiritual practice. This is one form of spiritual practice that can absolutely assist your development if you choose to apply it. However it is not meant to replace your current practices and exercises; it is meant to compliment them. Consistency is the key! **So please by all means fall in love with your spiritual practices. Treat them as you would your dearest friend.** The innocence you behold in your baby pictures is there within you even now.*

Allow this thought of who you really are to break your heart wide open and let your heart be moistened by the ocean of Love that is within you. You are not the ego, or the issues. You are the beloved and most sacred child and you

manifested out of the source of infinite good. Please contemplate this deeply and let the tears of innocence pour through you. Stay here for a little while. Don't rush through it. As you look at your baby pictures and remember who you really are, hug them and hold them close to your heart. Smile at them. Behold the image and likeness of Love and Perfect Beauty! Your own unique and universal energy is in that photo you are looking at. You are looking at the only picture that is exactly like this in the entire cosmos. And if there does happen to be another picture just like this one in a parallel universe—just know that just makes you doubly adorable. Let the energy of gratitude saturate your mind as you contemplate that you are here with a great purpose and that is to bring more of your Innocence, Beauty and your Love into this world. Through Life's magnificence and brilliance you were formed. You are not just hugging any photograph. <u>You are re-connecting with a portion of yourself that was forgotten and thus abandoned by you so many years ago. You are right now in this moment reclaiming your beloved innocence.</u> Please realize and accept with all your heart that you are right now an expanded version of that same awesomeness. You are looking at a perfect reflection of pure benevolence. After you look at your baby pictures and reflect intensely, find a mirror and gaze deeply into your eyes. As you stare into the windows of your soul and as the tears of Innocence pour through your being, say to yourself, "I am <u>Precious. I am Priceless. I am Beautiful and I am Adorable. I will never abandon my Innocence again.</u>" Through the language of Love, this is what your beloved tears are silently affirming.

Crying out to Love - Omni-Power!

As children we could make ourselves cry. We had true power! It was authentic power because it did not come from the outside of us. It came from the deepest and most sincere inner recesses of our hearts. We still have that same authentic and infinite power within us. As children we did not seek **the love of power,** we effortlessly exercised **the power of love.** It is very important to make this distinction. Many people associate the word power with something worldly; however it is time to revisit this concept. For worldly power is not true power at all and can never be greater than the Omnipotent power of the Spirit within. When Tears are shed that have emerged out of the source of Divine Love, they are indeed **All-Powerful / FULL OF OMNI POWER!** A child that is crying out to Love is a perfect example of what true power is all about. When we learn how to invoke and create the energy of Love like we did as children, then and only then have we truly become empowered. **The ability to create reality means absolutely nothing, if it is not the reality of Love. You don't get any spiritual props for being able to manifest worldly possessions. Even people that are on the path of greed and selfishness can manifest. In fact, the gift of manifesting done with an unhealthy motive can be a great liability to humanity, especially if it is void of spiritual wisdom and compassion. Worldly power that is not rooted in the infinite power of Love for those who have reclaimed their Innocence is a form of great weakness.**

When you were a child you were indeed a powerful being and it had nothing to do with your possessions or your accomplishments. Your greatest possessions then were your Innocence, your Beauty and your Love. Your greatest possessions even now are still Innocence, Beauty and Love. Please remember this. Embracing this attitude will help you attain true spiritual power particularly now that the awareness of who you really are is expanding. *Please know this beloved friend.* **We can invoke the Power of Love simply by making it a regular practice to cry out to Love with the full strength of our hearts.** Please always remember and affirm that your first spiritual teacher was You! You already taught yourself how to cry out to Love long ago. Contemplate the remembrance of your beloved child hood tears and they will spontaneously re-emerge. **With my own eyes, I have seen some of society's so-called hardest-hearted men transform into the gentlest and softest-hearted beings. This was after having their egos crushed and drowned by the unstoppable power of their very own tears.** Within us all is a great and endless ocean of

Grace. I am telling you, your tears possess miraculous and super-natural healing power! The flood gates of your heart must re-open. The experience of bliss is the goal of every opened heart. The adult ego has a divine destiny to die. Drown it in the ocean of your very own beloved tears.

The Resurrection Power contained in Mary Magdalena's' Beloved Tears

Some time back, people marveled over whether or not Mary Magdalene was Jesus' wife and that was perhaps a possibility. **However, when I researched our beloved sister's journey, what astonished me the most about Mary is the power that was contained in her tears.** Let me explain. In the book of John it says that Mary Magdalena's devotion and Love for Jesus was so strong that she stood outside of his tomb all alone

—weeping intensely—in hopes to discover where they had laid her beloved Jesus. She longed to re-unite with her precious Rabbi and Messiah and for the presence of his Love to consume her once again.

John 20:11 Now Mary stood outside the tomb *crying*. As she wept, she bent over to look into the tomb and saw two angels in white, seated where Jesus' body had been, one at the head and the other at the foot.

This is so powerful! Her Innocence and devotional crying had the power to invoke the presence of angelic beings! Then the passage goes on to say:

"They asked her, 'Woman, why are you *crying?*' 'They have taken my Lord away, and I don't know where they have put him.' At this, she turned around and saw Jesus standing there, but she did not realize it was him. Jesus then asked her the same question the angels did, 'Woman, why are you *crying*? Who is it you are looking for?'"

Did you notice that both the angels and Jesus asked Mary the same thing? They both asked Mary **why she was crying! They both recognized the infinite power of Mary's Innocence. Mary's tears had the power to pull Light beings out of other dimensions and cause Love to take a form.** Mary wept for Jesus in the same way a child or animal weeps when they have lost something that they love. I know this experience first-hand. My Grandma Mary died when I was nine and she was cherished and adored by me just as all Grandmothers are adored and cherished by their Grandchildren. Grandma was my all in all. In short, to me Grandma was God! For many years after she passed on to the next realm, I agonizingly cried blissful tears very regularly longing and hoping that Grandma would one day soon return. My tears were not in vain. In fact, they were so strong that years later I ended up being consumed and saturated by the presence of the Divine Mother who millions around the world affectionately and innocently call Amma.* I know the blissful pain of longing for someone you adore and Love very well. What I am revealing to you about Mary Magdalena's experience is not my belief or philosophy. I cried and longed for Jesus 2,000 years ago and Mary Magdalena cried and longed for my Grandma 2,000 years later. Our tears emerged from the same source. That source is your beloved heart of Innocence.

The pain of Mary being separated from her beloved caused her to experience deep agony and intense loneliness. Her longing was a longing for divine love. Her tears which were filled with the energy of perfect devotion had the power to invoke the presence of perfect Love or shall we say to bring Jesus back to Life. Her undying courage and dedication to stand alone at that tomb and pour her heart out to Love inspires and moves me in a much deeper way than if she was Jesus' wife or not. Mary Magdalena was indeed truly married. In this my heart has perfect faith. Mary was married to the inexhaustible energy of divine Love. She lived a life style of innocence, beauty and love and this was rooted in perfect devotion. She had an irresistible and everlasting preciousness about her that has compelled my heart to fall deeper in Love with her spirit every time I contemplate Mary's perfect example. She refused to waver until her crying manifested its desired result which was to invoke the presence of her beloved Lord. Does this ideal not touch, move and inspire you? We all have this exact same invocation power and capacity within us. We just have to cry out to Love just as we did as children and the angels (light-workers) will most definitely manifest. This is a natural and universal law. The consciousness of divine love is compelled to respond to the call of an innocent heart. I dare you to put this divine truth to the test.

For years people have interpreted this story and given the credit for Jesus' resurrection solely to Him or to Consciousness in the form of the Heavenly Father. However, was it not Mary Magdalene's Innocence and her intense maternal devotion and the power contained in her beloved tears that invoked the Christ Consciousness and compelled it to take another form? Beloved friend —through the power contained in your Innocence and tears—you can and you will— bring the dead spiritual state of humanity back to life.

Please affirm this thought ...

The perfect and omnipotent power that is within both you and I has the capacity and divine function to invoke the LOVE PRESENCE that pervades the entire creation. Now that's miraculous and true resurrection power! When our tears emerge out of us, it is the greatest evidence that we have aligned and become one with Universal Consciousness (God). Please accept this with all your heart.

The Sacred Waters Within

Water is one of the first forms that Spirit manifests as on this side of reality. When the Love within you cries out and your tears begin to flow, you have literally tapped the source of everlasting Life. It is a scientific fact that all water seeks itself (source). Your tears that have come from the eternal source within your very own being seek sacred union with sacred waters that reside within the heart of humanity and God. Your tears can therefore be likened to the rivers that flow towards the great lakes and oceans. There is an unexplainable/ mystical energy contained in each one of your tear drops. I absolutely dare you to cry out to Love just as you did when you were a child. You do have this capacity. You are still that same priceless and most precious beloved child. Your tears contain infinite power! Please use them to invoke the pure Omnipotent (All-powerful) Love that you were then and still are even now.

Yet...

At some point in our growth and development, something happened that caused a shift to occur. We went from living in and out of our hearts of innocence (power), to conforming to the dry and desert like existence that is fostered by our tainted adult perceptions of reality. When we lost touch with the home of our hearts, we began our journey through the Land of Oz (external love and illusion), hoping to find a wizard (spiritual teacher) that would help us find our way back home. Searching for Love in the external world brought us much internal pain. We found some spiritual teachers, all right! They were the spiritual teachers known as hurt, pain, and let down and these things would eventually assist us in becoming open and receptive enough to finally be willing, like Dorothy, to "click our *heals*" (begin our healing process), close our eyes, and turn our energy inward. Let's face it. Life and the pangs of Life itself have oftentimes for us become the teacher of all teachers.

We all know this pain very well, don't we? There is no need to go into detail about it. Who does not know what it feels like to be let down by the search for love in the external world?

Place your hand on your heart, close your eyes and repeat the sacred mantra "There's no place like home. There is no place like home." Do this as many times as you like. This home, beloved, is your very own heart. As you place your hand on your heart, please pay attention to the selfless vibration of your heartbeat. Your heart is selflessly pumping blood (love) throughout your body. Your heart loves you and through its selfless beating is reminding you who you really are—the vibration of an endless love.

Someone's Beloved Child

You are someone's beloved child and that someone is the essence of all Life. Sages come to the earth in innocence, simply to help us remember that we are all that very same innocence deep within. You came to this earth for that very purpose as well. That child you, that innocent you, that wise you, and that aware you, is that sage.

A great Master once said, *"Unless you become like children (Innocent), you will not enter the kingdom of heaven (Love)."*

Jesus' profoundly brilliant, yet most simple words of power, capture the essence of everything this book is conveying. He also said that the kingdom of heaven (Love) was within us, not something to be searched for in the world outside. Once this innocence within is rediscovered, reawakened, realized, and reclaimed, the greatest dream of all dreams comes true. We once again, like we did as children, live life in and out of the fullness and depth of the heart which is where Jesus said the King's treasure is. *"For where your treasure is, there your heart will be also."*

Once we discover this priceless treasure within, we realize that the journey through the land of illusions (Oz) was a needed part of our spiritual development. We are able then to smile at and even have a deep and sincere appreciation for the entire journey no matter how painful it may have been. Are you open to this beautiful possibility? You must be if you are reading this. Your openness, no matter how small or large it may be, is evidence that Love, God, and Infinite Beauty are there within you. Your heart is expanding. **You are spiritually growing and thus all the innocent beings (the angels) throughout the boundless universe are dancing and celebrating.**

It is not that you are reading something spiritual that measures your spiritual development. It is how open your heart remains. **Children are open.** You are open now, which means that you have in this moment transformed into a beloved child and have thus begun the process of reclaiming your power of innocence!

The Beloved and Universal Child Is the Teaching and the Teacher, and the Child's Technique Is Free!

When we were children, life was beautiful simply because we did not critically analyze everything. We were not attached to having to understand or know it all. Like spiritual sponges, we just absorbed Life and Life absorbed us. We lived in a state of yoga (union). As children we lived in a state of yogic bliss simply because our hearts were not just open, they were *wide* open. This was the reality we all held in common once upon a time. As children we did not need any self-help books, a meditation technique, or spiritual teachings to help us attain this state of openness. We *were* the spiritual teaching that everyone learned from and wanted to be. **We were all indeed incarnations of the Universal Child.** Our every action was the Spiritual Masters technique. Simply being who we were as children, effortlessly, brought joy into the lives of all who were in our presence. We were the center of attention simply because Love is at the center of everything good.

As children we embodied love. This state of consciousness did not cost us a dime. At some point in our lives, something happened so inwardly tragic that we came to believe that we had to *pay* (with money or through penance) for an experience that would help us to become something that we already were and already are. Many people have thus said, **"I spent thousands of dollars going to seminars searching for Love, and I finally came to see that Love was inside of me**

and all the time it was free." Wow! The tragedy was that we forgot our innocence—however that happened—so we could inherit wisdom. Life is always for us and never against us. Good can be extracted out of every situation if we are determined to find it.

"I know that my true nature is Love, and not because of something that I read in a book. I know my true nature is Love simply because I remember who I was as a child. Today I am just an expanded version of that same child." Remind yourself of this frequently. Do you see how simple this is? Become a child again. Without this openness of heart, nothing on the spiritual path can be attained or realized.

You can't pay for Love,but you can –Offer it

How can you pay for your true nature? Love is the essence of whom and what we already are. Love is free, just like your Life was when you were born and just like your Life is even now. Life freely brought you into this world simply for the sake of Love and because of its ever-liberated nature. Every time you breathe you experience Love and its super-abundant state of infinite freedom. And please remember that the air we breathe comes to us free of charge. Many people today pay thousands of dollars going to spiritual seminars and transformational retreats, desperately hoping that their hearts might once again re-open. They believe that they have lost something—yet the only thing they have lost is the awareness of who they really are; *little beloved children.*

The willingness to spend our hard-earned money on our spiritual development is all good. We purchase food at the grocery store; how much more important is our spiritual food? Awareness here is the key! When you pay for anything regarding your conscious development, make it an offering of love and not a payment. Share it with an intention that is selfless. This Love offering will support your spiritual evolution. Share your money like a child would share his or her new toy with his or her friends. Offer your money in innocence. It then becomes more than money you earned, but love-energy you shared. Your money then will get converted into universal power!

A Child Forever

The world taught you that you were an adult, but spiritually you will always be someone's beloved child. **In the world you are born, and will eventually grow old and die. In the Spirit, you awaken, expand in consciousness and live forever as a child of love in the eternal now.** I do not care how many wrinkles show up on your face, or how many gray hairs may be popping up. Even when our bodies beg to differ, spiritually we will always be little beloved children. This should help us relax just a little.

Growing in Awareness

Instead of expanding in the awareness of the innocence, love, and infinite beauty that we are, we oftentimes fall deeper into a state of spiritual sleep. This happens because of our addiction to searching for external images of love in all their illusory forms.

When you become aware that your search for love in the external world can never bring you true fulfillment, you have grown in spiritual wisdom. It confirms that your awareness has expanded and that you are indeed spiritually evolving. It may be painful to finally have to come to terms with this reality, but please remember that through the womb of this pain a new you is being born again.

It is not enough to develop the power of innocence. **This innocence must be grounded in wisdom, discernment and discrimination.** Your life's experiences have indeed given you wisdom. **However you must be totally honest with yourself to access this wisdom.** Accept and celebrate this. If you study your own life with an open heart, you will come to see that it is indeed as sacred as any other scripture. **Your life itself is the Word and Wisdom of God and really the only self-help book you ever need to read. I am not telling you not to read other sacred text and books. That would be silly. What I am saying is to remember that when you are reading any sacred text that you are reading about yourself.** As my cherished friend of humanity and spiritual mentor Michael Bernard

Beckwith has so beautifully said, "**The answer is you!**"

A Child's Mind Is a Universe

As children, it was not important to know that we lived in a boundless universe; our minds *were* the boundless universe! Try this on and see how it feels. Drop the egoistic title of *adult.* **Now inwardly accept and embrace with your total being that you are, right now in this moment, an infinitely precious child who has acquired spiritual wisdom. Your mind is as expansive as the universe and it is a universe! You have an entire universe within and without to play in, to grow in, and most importantly, to love in. Your life has been written by the very hand of divine love. Your story is just as sacred and important as any scripture that has ever been revealed. You are a Book of Life. This is reality. All life is sacred and** precious. **Your Life is sacred and precious. Have the courage to embrace this and the openness to accept it.**

A life of innocence, love, and beauty can be reclaimed! This is good news, and the technique to rediscovering this innocence, love, and beauty will not cost you one cent. It is as free as the air we all breathe and the sun rays that shine on us all. The technique is as simple as the thumping of your heartbeat and as selfless as your exhale. This technique is already there within you and it is activated simply by first remembering and accepting with all of your heart that you are someone's beloved child and that someone is Love. I know the complicated "adult intellectual and analytical you" may want it to be more difficult than that, but remember: The things of the heart are very, very simple. Life is also very simple. You inhale and you exhale. As a matter of fact, let's stop right here for a moment and take a few conscious deep breaths so we can experience first-hand how beautiful and simple life really is.

Nothing in this world can afford to purchase your soul

I have spoken to so many people along my spiritual journey who have told me that they felt empty inside, almost as if they had lost their very own hearts and souls. When I was young and had lost so many of my childhood friends to brutal murder, my heart went numb. The Love inside my heart and soul was still there, it was just frozen and needed to be thawed out. You cannot lose your own heart and soul, beloved, but it can certainly feel that way. It may even feel as if you have sold it for the luxuries and material things in life, but I've got news for you, my friend: Your soul is infinitely costly! No one in the universe could ever afford to buy your soul, so you might as well get over that nonsense. **All the wealth of the world is mere rubbish when compared to the eternal wealth of your soul.** You have not lost one bit of your heart and soul's love.

Your soul, your heart, and your love are not for sale and could not be afforded by absolutely anything in this world. **You are the Eternal Wealth of God!** My beloved Amma once said this to all Her devotees and I ran with it! **I AM THE ETERNAL WEALTH OF GOD!** No one could ever tell me anything to make me accept any other truth because this is divine truth! **Every last one of us is indeed the ETERNAL Wealth of God! All the wealth of the world bows to the feet of the child (angelic being) who has realized their eternal wealth.** Your child-like beauty is infinitely priceless! The fleeting wealth of the world is longing to align itself with the eternal wealth of your heart. There is great wisdom contained in this statement. Please do not take this to be philosophical jargon that only sounds good. Have you ever noticed that spiritual masters never do any money affirmations or very rarely even speak of it – yet they always have all the resources they need to accomplish their missions? Have you ever contemplated and asked your heart why this is? I have! Their perfected state of being is ever full of wealth-consciousness, and it is a wealthy state of being that is not defined or tainted by the world's limited version of what it *believes* wealth really is. The world defines wealth as having to do with finances or material resources *only*—and because those things are fleeting—to the Great Masters they are not to be defined as true wealth. The fleeting wealth of the world bows to the feet of the eternal wealth of the heart not the other way around. Now here is the key, beloved. God is the owner of everything good and consciousness is ever full of itself. All the wealth and resources of the world therefore belongs to God or shall we say to the children of God. All worldly and also spiritual wealth belongs to God and God resides in the temple of your heart—all the wealth that is— or ever will be—is therefore already there within you. **You are truly the eternal wealth of God** if you only but knew it! All the wealth of the world surrenders at your feet once you become aware of who you really are. So share the riches and wealth of your heart freely and watch how the wealth of the world proves to you that you own it. All of this is tied into you reclaiming your Innocence. Only a heart that is filled with Innocence will get this.

Please remember this

Here is good example to bring this point home. The perfect Innocence of the baby Jesus (the sacred child) attracted the presence of wise men (humanity) who offered their wealth at the Baby King's feet. You all remember the story. The wise men brought gold, frankincense and myrrh which all represented some form of spiritual and worldly wealth and riches. They say Jesus was born poor; however, that is a spiritual misnomer. Jesus was born eternally rich simply because he incarnated fully aware of who he really was. Jesus did not have to do any wealth affirmations—yet by the time he was two, the worldly wealth needed to carry out his mission was on the way! The reason that the unaware say that Jesus was poor is because they are using the standards of a spiritually broke and ignorant world to interpret his legacy. To be Christ-Conscious is to accept and embrace and also realize that you are indeed THE ETERNAL WEALTH OF GOD! **"ALL THE WEALTH OF THE WORLD BOWS TO MY FEET. IT LONGS TO BE USED BY ME SELFLESSLY. I AM THE ETERNAL WEALTH OF GOD!"**

Your childhood memories are priceless

Take a few moments right now to reflect on one of your beloved and priceless childhood memories. This will greatly complement the spiritual practice of focusing your attention on your baby pictures. You may have to dig deep to find that diamond (the wealth within), but there is indeed a **benevolent** childhood experience within you to be remembered and treasured. **Painful memories may be there as well, but please consider that this pain can be used by you to give your character spiritual luster and depth.** So dig, beloved reader. Dig until you find your inner diamond and auspicious childhood experience.

The Sacred Womb of Your Heart

The spiritual path is only for the courageous! **If situations that you consider negative and painful continue to arise, do your best to tell yourself what this has taught you and how you have grown from it. Remember also that millions of people in this world have suffered and you are not alone. Look for ways in which your childhood experiences of hurt have made you more compassionate. You now can understand the pain and suffering of others and are perfectly qualified to Love and serve an ailing humanity. Looking at things this way will not only help you heal, but will also help you develop spiritual depth. This world is in great need of spiritual depth and compassion.** Find your inner pearl experience, write it down on paper, and contemplate it deeply. What you are writing down is as sacred as any scripture that has ever been written. Your life story is the sacred song of the Divine. Please remember this. And please know that God has many more songs to sing through you. You have an infinite amount of songs inside you. Those songs, beloved, are your very own – **sacred scriptures**. Share them with this hurting world and allow your divine music to heal the heart of humanity.

Remember your new and improved, yet very simple affirmation and mantra: **"There is no place like the home of my heart."** This is very simple, yet very profound. True spiritual practice is very simple.* When your mind tries to complicate this process, simply place your hand on your heart and repeat the sacred mantra, **"I am a beloved child and my inner and outer beauty is** priceless. **There is no place like the home of my heart."** Again, if any pain emerges, remember that every mother who gives birth to a child experiences tremendous pain. Your heart is just like an ever-expanding womb and sacred space. A new you will be birthed through the pain of this most sacred space if you let it. **Not only do you have a most lovable and universal child within you, you also have an all-loving Mother and Sacred and all-faithful Father within that loves that child unconditionally. Our parents may have hurt us tremendously, and this is why we must empower ourselves by re-creating the divine family within.** It's okay. Do not run from the pain. Allow the new you to come through. This is something that we all must do. You are absolutely never alone.

A Dream I Had as a Child

When I was a child, my dream was to one day move to Hong Kong and become a student of Bruce Lee. At the age of about 8, I even began giving Karate lessons to my friends and they were all willing to come to Hong Kong with me to find our beloved Kung Fu Master Bruce Lee.

I was so absorbed in this vision that many times instead of going to school I would sneak downtown and sit in the Kung Fu movie theater all day long. I never thought about how much money it would cost for me to one day travel to Hong Kong to be tutored by Bruce Lee, nor did I doubt my dream one bit. I lived in a state of awareness that told me that everything my mind's eye envisioned had already happened! I pretended that I was Bruce Lee all the time. This was one of the realities that I chose to live in.

Little did I know that Bruce Lee had already left his body in 1973. It was in 1977 that I developed this vision and, as far as I was concerned, Bruce Lee was alive and living strong inside the world of my heart's dream. If no one had told me that he had died, or had I never discovered it on my own, it would not have mattered. Training with Bruce Lee was already occurring within the deathless and undefeated world of my heart.

Due to the heaviness of life's hurts and my lack of knowledge of how to deal with them, my childhood dream disappeared. I remember the moment very clearly that triggered all of my pain. It was when my father discovered that I was playing hooky from school to go watch those Kung Fu movies. Instead of embracing me with Love and talking with me, he did not let me express myself—and he also slapped me very hard in the face. He slapped my dream right out of existence! I was a child and had no knowledge of reclaiming my power.

Prior to living with my father, I was emotionally and physically abused by my mother and stepfather. When I moved with my father, it was a great relief for me and I trusted him to protect me. When he hit me, it was like the entire universe hit me! At that point I turned to the streets (the Land of Oz) for counsel, guidance, and love. When my heart became filled with pain and resentment, my childhood vision to one day study with Bruce Lee vanished. It was not because Bruce Lee had passed on; it was because the innocence of my heart had. Wow...

If you take the time to contemplate your childhood experiences, you will remember that you too once had a fearless dream. As a child you were spontaneously absorbed in a dream world of wonder that you, yourself created. As a child you had power! And this power's source was your very own heart. It is not necessary to rediscover your childhood dream unless it is still important to you; perhaps that dream was supposed to pass. Let it go and reclaim its source! This Source is the essence of love, innocence, and beauty that you still are even now. This infinitely powerful source is within your very own heart and is indeed as selfless as your very own heartbeat!

I adore you tremendously.

Love, Temba Spirit

* *After having this revelation while writing this section of the book, I spontaneously created a Facebook page inviting people to post their baby pictures:*
(*http://www.facebook.com/InternationalBabyPictureDay*).
Baby pictures are popping up on it every day. It's so sweet.

*I will reveal more of my experiences with my Grandma Mary and my beloved Amma in my book, **A Mother in a man's body:** *Honoring the Maternal Aspects of God* and also in my book, **The Compassion of a convicted felon:** *When a prison cell becomes the heart of God.*

• **The simple spiritual exercises that I have suggested in this book are not meant to, by any means, replace the practices that you already** have. They are only suggestions that can complement your personal development.

Chapter 2

The Inexhaustible Power of Selfless Love

"And this is the destiny of the fortunate. Love is the fortune of the fortunate. The Abundance of Love is the goal of all destiny. Fortunate are the ones whose hearts flow in Love."

—Maharishi Mahesh Yogi

Do your absolute best not to be obsessively attached to the discovery of your life purpose, destiny and dream. When you tap back into the innate innocence, beauty, and Love that you truly are, through this portal of Life and awareness, your purpose will effortlessly reveal itself. It is

110

your obsessive attachment to the discovering of your Life purpose that can potentially create clouds that will block the sunlight of your purpose and destiny. No one but you can create these clouds. And no one but you can remove them. This is the good news! It is important to not view these clouds as bad, as they represent an essential lesson in the grand scheme of Life's purpose.

You can also create clouds that cover the sunlight of your destiny by comparing your success to others, complaining and whining, not appreciating Life, and also by not being totally happy when you notice someone who is living a fulfilled life. Harboring envy and jealousy will definitely cover over your innocence and beauty, as well as create these same clouds. Always remember that you are the creator of the clouds. Looking at it this way will empower you.

Being the creator of these clouds means that you can also be their destroyer! Becoming aware is the key! Remember that clouds pass, and that the sunshine is always shining even when it appears that it is not. Your life's purpose is always shining infinitely strong—you just have to remove the clouds. It's all about your attitude! Do your best not to compromise having a good attitude. Place some gratitude in your attitude and your life's purpose will gain altitude! This is a spiritual guarantee!

It Is All Coming from You

The essence of any worthy Life purpose is the abundant and overflowing experience and sharing of Love. Now this is an empowering attitude to take! With this attitude you cannot go wrong. The abundance and overflowing of Love is the essence of all true Life Purpose, and it can be compared to endless sunshine. Imagine Love! Believe Love! Trust Love! Accept Love! Embrace Love! Share Love! Love is the only thing that makes life meaningful.

When the Love that is deep within us comes to the surface of Life, our universal purpose to Love is *exhaled* into the world. You are infinitely beautiful within and without. There is a limitless supply of Love within you. I love remembering how beautiful you are; however, I cannot *reclaim* your inner beauty for you. You have to reclaim, realize, and remember it yourself. That is why this book is called *How to* Reclaim **Your** Innocence! No one can reclaim your beauty, love, and innocence for you, just as no one can breathe for you. We can remind each other of it, but it is you that must reclaim it. **We can lead the horse to the Lake of Love, but we cannot make that horse drink the water once it gets there.**

I am also aware that I could not acknowledge your inner and outer beauty unless I had it myself—just as you could not acknowledge my beauty unless you had it yourself. Every time you acknowledge something beautiful, something pleasant, something profound, etc., also acknowledge that this awareness is coming from you first and foremost.

People go to visit gurus, spiritual teachers, and transformational personalities, and they leave saying, *"So and so was so beautiful and enlightened!"*—but then they turn around and speak something negative about themselves. There is nothing humble about that, nor is that authentic. **Remember the platinum and universal rule: You cannot genuinely acknowledge something that you are not also yourself!** Please remember this and apply it to how you see life. You will be amazed at how a simple shift of awareness such as this can enhance the overall quality of your life.

You Are as Selfless as the Sun Rays; Keep It Simple

Love is ever-free, selfless, and not attached to anything, just like sun rays are not. Do you accept this? If you do, that means that this selfless Love I am talking about is coming from you. As I said, you could not genuinely acknowledge it unless you indeed had it yourself. Do you see how simple this is? **You just have to practice this awareness exercise moment to moment and fall in love with this ideal.**

Sun rays have one essence intention, and that is to selflessly shine. They love to be free and so do we, right? Our essence purpose is the same as sunshine—*freedom*. We both love to shine and we both love to be free! The difference is the sun can shine with or without you. **We have to learn** to shine with or without knowing what the specifics of our life purpose are. Just imagine how life would be if the sun waited to figure out the details each day before it decided to shine. There would be no life purpose for us to even consider. All of our lives are dependent on the magnificent Life purpose of the sun that shines daily. This thought absolutely humbles me.

The Many Life Purposes That Make It Possible for Us to Shine!

Our life purpose is dependent on a whole bunch of other life purposes being intact. We seem to miss that when we consider what our life purpose may or may not be. Each and every last one of the life purposes that support us give to us freely. Therefore, be free like the sun rays and give selflessly like the air. Shine your light and love into and on the world with a selfless intention. **Fall in Love with the ideal of selfless love. Contemplate selfless love. Open your heart and willingly offer it to the power of selfless love. Do your best not to try hard to be selfless. Love does not try to be. Love just is what it is. Your nature is selfless love. And I can prove it using a very simple example.**

The Breath of Life – Purpose

Every time you breathe you have no other choice but to selflessly exhale a breath back into the world. You share a selfless breath with the world every time you exhale. You selflessly give carbon dioxide to the trees and plants and they selflessly give oxygen back to you. You are a selfless being, like it or not. Everything in creation gives in this way. You are not separate from the system of selflessness that permeates Life. You are an important part of it!

You cannot take back your last breath, can you? Your very nature is selfless love. Selflessness is manifesting its energy through you even without you knowing it. However, if you want to know what selfless love is, simply observe your own breathing, your heartbeat, and the blinking of your very own eyes.

I told you that your very life was as sacred as any scripture. Study yourself by observing your simple nature and you will be studying universal law. It's really that easy, especially once you fall in Love with the purpose of Life itself which is to Love, be Loved, and become Love.

Through your breathing alone, you are a selfless being. And just as you do not have to try to breathe, you do not have to *try* to be selfless. You give selflessly to life all the time. **We just simply have to become aware.** You have to give to live!

Selfless love is your truest nature. Every time you breathe you experience your own love supreme. Do you accept and embrace this with your whole heart, beloved reader? Every spiritual lesson in life can be learned by the patient observation and study of our very own breath of Life. It's all oh so simple.

Your Dream Wants to Be Free. Free It!

The thing that is creating the bondage in your life is the very thing that (once a slight shift of awareness occurs) can also create your freedom. But just like you must let go of your breath in order to live, *this thing*, this concept, this obsessive attachment known as your life's purpose must also be surrendered to life and let go of as well. Contemplate this, beloved. The nature of the universe is freedom! Your first nature is freedom! You are not separate from the universe. You are a part of it and *are* it! Everything about you wants total freedom and this includes your very life purpose, vision, and dream.

When we are out of alignment with this awareness all that is left is mental, emotional, and spiritual incarceration. Do your best not to incarcerate your dreams and visions, beloved. I know so many people who are miserable because they are obsessed with discovering their purpose and they just cannot seem to find it. It is so sad. The very thing that can free them has them in bondage. But, really, it is they who are holding themselves and their purpose captive. They have to learn to exhale (let go, release). They are holding their dream captive and sabotaging their own destiny. Their life purpose is there within them. They just have it imprisoned by their own minds. They will blame all of life's circumstances and make a thousand excuses but really it is they who have created the clouds that are blocking the sunlight of their life purpose.

You Can Incarcerate Your Spiritual Power and You Can Also Release It

Indeed, we all have the power to incarcerate our own spiritual power simply by choosing to mentally cling to things that want to be free. Your vision, dream, destiny and purpose want to be free just like the sunshine, your heartbeat, and your breath! **They even want to be free from you!** Love will remain imprisoned in our hearts until we release (free) it. Remember your dream knows who and what it is even if you don't. Free that dream inside you by letting go of the idea of whatever it may or may not be. **Your dream is like a universal boomerang; it will return to you when you hurl it out into the stars** and trust Love. **When it returns to you, continue releasing it by sharing it with everyone!** Love it enough to let it go by sharing it with the world and you will see the magic of your Life Purpose unfold.

Offer Your Life Purpose to Love

Clinging to anything, including the thought of what your Life's purpose and gift may or may not be, is spiritually unhealthy. We need a healthy relationship with Spirit (Essence-Love) in order to be aligned with an ever-free universe and its support. **Keep remembering that you are a beloved child and stay aware of the free gift of your breathing.**

The passion and purpose of the universe is to support you in everything good; however, you must first re-awaken the love essence within to align with this support. This is not as hard as it may seem. All it takes is the innocent faith of a mustard seed and your heart's willingness to surrender by offering your life's purpose—whatever it may be—to love. Remember that in order to live you must receive and give, receive and give, etc. Remember that you are the vessel of Life Purpose and not its owner.

As I already said, a good place to start is to become aware of the selfless breath of life that breathes love through you in every moment. Accept this with openness and innocence and true spiritual experience will indeed happen for you.

Love wants to know that you want it (Love) even more than you want the details of your Life purpose. This point is extremely important. In other words, if you never discovered the specifics of your Life purpose, would you still Love and appreciate your life? Even if your mind says no, be victorious with your heart's energy and say YES! Do whatever it takes to remain in this **YES awareness** and the details of your Life's purpose will surrender at your feet. This is a spiritual guarantee!

Your Life's Purpose is not somewhere out there beneath the pale moon-light. It is right here with you, through you, and around you. You are the Light and your light is not pale in the least bit. It is bright and vibrant! When you surrender your Life purpose to love, Love surrenders its Life purpose to you. To do this is to align with all-goodness. Please do not underestimate how powerful a practice this is. Just keep watching your breath. Every time you inhale and exhale you are surrendering and offering your life purpose to Love. We must inhale life and exhale (let go of) life or we die. We equally must

124

surrender our purpose to Love, or it dies. So simple, yet so profound this is. Surrendering to love is the sweetest victory. Not just for you, but for everything good that ever has or will ever exist.

So many people as they are searching for Purpose do not realize that the search for Life purpose is in no way separate from the discovery. The search and the journey to Purpose is your Purpose! **Your purpose is seeking you while you think you are seeking it. Love longs to embody you. It is when we surrender our thoughts, desires, and the search of purpose to love that we realize that our Life's purpose is contained within every breath that we take.** The *essence* of all Purpose has to be first realized. Once you tap the essence of your purpose, which is the Love and Beauty that you really are, the details of your purpose will effortlessly reveal themselves.

I adore you just as you are.

Love, Temba Spirit

Chapter 3

The Supreme Power of Stillness and Silence

"Even a stone, and more easily a flower or a bird, could show you the way back to God, to the Source, to yourself. When you look at it or hold it & let it be without imposing a word of mental label on it, a sense of awe, of wonder, arises within you. Its essence silently communicates itself to you and reflects your own essence back to you. This is what great artists sense and succeed in conveying in their art."

—Eckhart Tolle

Many people are searching for their purpose—but really they are searching for what is on the *surface level* of their purpose, thinking that they are searching for the *root* of their purpose. They are searching for the chatter of their purpose and not its source, which is stillness and silence. **Your purpose is not to be found in the noisy complicated details of life. Your purpose is to be realized in the sweet and simple surrender of silence (meditation).** Your life purpose, which is always some precious form of Love, will emerge spontaneously out of the deep silence within once you surrender and your being becomes still.

There is no specific technique for surrendering and offering that is better than the next one. The one that works for you is the best one for you. *Offering* is a conscious decision that we all must make if we want to expand in universal consciousness. It is a great gift that we receive from Life and its Purpose when we realize that it is the seed and root of purpose that must come first, not its branches and the leaves. Ironically when we offer our purpose to Life and Love, we are aligning in the greatest way with our purpose. When we return to the silence and stillness within, this is an authentic and effective way to align with the **root of our Life Purpose** and offer our lives to Love.

Many of us want the branches, leaves, and fruit of purpose to manifest without first planting the seed of purpose and thoroughly nurturing its root. **Please stop for a second and contemplate this**. The root grows out of the silence and depth of the earth (the heart). And the root breaks forth out of the seed of Love. The seed of purpose is Love, the root of purpose is Love, the trunk, the branches, the leaves and the fruit all have a purpose to Love, to give, and to serve. There is a divine order to the whole process. **When we align with this natural process we are now thinking with the organically inclined and divine mind.** We then will attract the entire support of Mother Nature who is the teacher of all teachers.

We Are Nature

The most profound personalities in the transformational world all have to surrender to the breath of Life that Mother Nature provides. She provides the seeds that we plant. Without Mother Nature there is no transformational world or any spiritual techniques. That is the bottom line. Becoming spiritually aware is to learn to listen closer to what She is telling us through her the silence and Her beauty. Not nature only outside of us, nature also inside of us. We are Nature! When She speaks to us through the silence, She is speaking to Herself.

The Tree of Life – Purpose

Have you taken the time to plant the seed of Love deep within your heart (earth) by spending time in the silence? You have to become a spiritual Gardener. The best gardening of the heart is done in the silence and stillness of love. Once you plant those beloved seeds, you have to nurture them. You plant the seeds of Love with the intention of Love and you nurture the seed with the silence of Love. **The process to discovering your Life purpose is very organic.** In fact, this natural process is you, *as your Life purpose,* becoming more aware of itself. You are the Life Purpose that you are searching for. Isn't that so beautiful?

Absolutely everything that is happening to you, for you and through you *right now* is your life purpose becoming more aware of what and who it really is. Your Life purpose is therefore not something to discover in the future, but it is something to realize that is happening right now! **Please take a few moments and contemplate this.**

You have to get this, beloved. We often look for the details and a description of purpose, (the leaves and branches) instead of the root essence which is always realized in the silence and is right here within you and happening through you right now. **The more time you spend in the silence and stillness, the more the song of your purpose will sing itself through you and also into this beloved world.**

This is what all true Masters who have walked this earth have said in their own unique ways. This is how the master within me decided to say it on my song *Reclaim Your Power*: **"Everybody got a song inside them. Everybody got**

a gift that comes out of the silence." If we go out in nature and sit with the Trees of Life, through the silence of nature they will reveal true Life purpose. This is what the Buddha did. Siddhartha Gautama Buddha attained his enlightenment while sitting under a Tree of Life. Humanity was instructed to eat from a Tree of Life in the Garden of Eden. In the book of Revelation, it says that humanity will once again be able to eat from the Tree of Life. When the Lakota Native Americans Sun Dance, they return to the most sacred Tree of Life.

There is something very significant to what I am saying about The Tree of Life - Purpose. You can have all the purpose in the world, but if it is not rooted deeply, like the Tree of Life is rooted deeply in the silence of supreme love, you have absolutely nothing. That is the lesson that the Great Trees of Life (Spiritual Masters) teach us.

They are silent Love incarnate. The next time you see a Tree, remember your Tree of Life Purpose is to breathe silent Love in and exhale it back into this beloved world.

Silent Love

When you give from your whole heart and with your entire being, you then taste the state of silent love. When we serve with a pure motive, we are silent and still within. We are not thinking about love. We have become Love. There is no disturbance within. Not only is our love silent at that point, our Love with form is actually moving through the silence just like sound waves move through water. When we speak words of Beauty, Love, Compassion, Kindness, Integrity, and Understanding, our words (vibration and sound) are moving through the infinite space of silent Love. We become the divine paradox. We become the ever-moving vibration of Love as well as the ever-still silence of Love.

You Are Formless Love Watching Form

Love's source is not the mind; the mind's source is Love. The mind jumps back and forth like a monkey swinging on a vine, and unless we learn to watch it (which is how the monkey is tamed) our lives will just swing on the vine with it. The untamed monkey, the swing, and the vine are all beautiful forms of love that want to be tamed by the Master (the watcher, the witness, the awareness, the formless love) simply also known as the **Real You.** The monkey mind can, however, become the **enlightened monkey** if the swinging thoughts are allowed to sink back into the silence of Love. When we watch our thoughts and allow them to pass that is exactly what happens. Once the thoughts return to their source, they can re-emerge in victory!

Let me explain. You may be experiencing a thought of doubt. If you allow that thought to run its organic course and die in the silence without reacting to it, you can resurrect that same thought-vibration as a thought of trust, faith, and empowerment. You can literally inhale the negative thought (let it die) and exhale a positive one (bring it back to life). Our thoughts are just vibrations that have taken form. We can allow them to return to their source, which is the formless silence, and then use our power of choice to resurrect them in spiritual brilliance! You have to regularly practice this as a spiritual exercise to really get this. Those who take the time out to practice this simple exercise will accelerate their spiritual growth by spiritual leaps and esoteric bounds.

Thoughts are powerful; however, the source of our thoughts is the Parent of that Power! You are that parent, beloved reader. Take time out each day to simply watch your own thoughts. You will be amazed to discover that you are not *just* your thoughts—you are also their source.

Thoughts really have no meaning save the ones that we give them. **The reason why focusing on the breath of Life and your breathing is so powerful is because there is no thinking involved.** Like the river of love, there is just a constant and dynamic flow. That is why I suggested you breathe your negative thoughts away. If you focus on your breath and not your thoughts and mind, you are in the peace zone. That is indeed the place to be.

Your stress is caused by your reaction to your thinking. You are not thinking when you are watching your breath; you are witnessing and reclaiming your power! **"Everybody got a song inside them. Everybody got a gift that comes out of the silence."** *Just imagine!* You can dance and have fun and also spiritually rejuvenate your being by singing along with my song **Reclaim your Power**! What a great day and time we are living in! But please remember that a song is just a reminder, not the goal. Songs come and go, but silent Love is always there for the songs and gifts of Life to emerge out of.

The source of sound, thoughts, and the mind is silent Love. Learn to identify with the source of the mind. Once you begin being the "watcher" of your thoughts, you will, as I said, realize that you are not just your thoughts, you are also their source!

Enya Spirit –My beloved sister

Some may find the experience of silent love by contemplating nature's beauty. Some may reach this stillness by chanting their sacred mantra, praying, or singing songs to the Divine. Some may reach this place through deep contemplation. I sometimes like to just place my hand on my heart and marvel at its selfless beating while listening to **Enya** songs. I have never met Enya, but I have met her in my heart's silence. The sound of the heartbeat itself is a most sacred mantra and can very easily take you into a state of silent love if you are willing to let it. Ah—my heartbeat and my beloved sister Enya. Now that's silent love.

Others suggest, as I have, that we focus on our breath and watch it come in and out. And then there is my favorite: Crying tears of compassion on behalf of the suffering and then converting those tears into selfless action. Tears are silent Love incarnate, just like the Trees. Tears are liquid prayers and extremely powerful and subtle mantras. Whatever it takes for us to get to the stillness within is what we must do to stay there. When we dwell in that sacred place, we are free. We are not imprisoned by our thoughts, nor are our thoughts imprisoned by us.

A Mother's Love Is Meditation Incarnate

Mothers do not have to think about how to attain this state of silent love that I speak about. A mother's love is natural and 100% authentic. Every mother who is reading this knows exactly what I am talking about. Mothers love their children unconditionally and from a place of a silence that is deep within. So deep is the selfless and silent love of a mother that the image of the

Sacred Mother and child has been adored for thousands of years in various cultures throughout the world. The Madonna and child is the sacred symbol that represents the stillness, silence, and selflessness of love, also known as *meditation.*

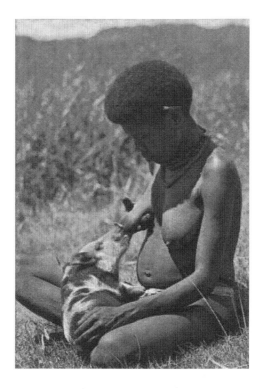

The Perfect image of Innocence, Selflessness and Silent Love (Meditation)

The Sacred Mother and child can be likened to the perfected state attained in meditation

The sacred child is eternally meditating in the lap of the Divine Mother. The breast milk that is nurturing the child is love moving through the stillness. The stillness is the immovable love that the mother has for the child. With this awareness, the beautiful essence and nature of all women should be adored.

Meditation is the practice that allows us to relax and also to re-align ourselves with our *essence nature*. A mother's unconditional love for her child is her super-organic meditative state that we all strive to attain on the spiritual path. Not only do we relax the body when we meditate, we also relax the thinking process of the mind. Mothers do not think when they are breastfeeding their children; the milk (which is the love) just flows.

To not think is to rest in perfect stillness. In the book of Genesis in the Bible it says that God rested on the seventh day. This seventh day is known as the Sabbath in the Hebrew tradition, however, many do not realize that the Sabbath or the seventh day of rest is not just a day; it is also a state of consciousness that can be attained through a regular heartfelt meditation practice. To rest in God Consciousness is to trust that all things are provided and taken care of. It is to align ourselves with the Divine Mind/Mother that effortlessly keeps all things in perfect harmony and universal balance. Meditation allows us to rest in the lap of the Universal Mother just as a child rests in the lap of its mother. **When we watch our thoughts come and go and do not cling to them, they attain liberation (freedom). We are then back in the lap of the Most Sacred Universal Mother.**

Thoughts come and go, do they not? Let them come and go. Underneath this coming and going is *awareness*. I like to call this perfect state of awareness the silence and stillness of a mother's unconditional love.

We rest the body, but how many of us have learned how to rest the mind? The mind wants to rest in the sacred lap of its Mother/essence. We rest the body so that it functions at its highest capacity, and we rest the brain for the same reason.

When we love and serve others with a selfless intention, we are bringing relaxation to our entire being just as the universal Mother brings rest to all beings when they approach her with Innocence. To have a selfless intention is to let go of trying to control the outcome of our service. To let go is to relax. It is to exhale. It is to value peace of mind over anything else. This is why the power of Love is so liberating. It is really very simple. It is all about learning to relax. When a mother is breastfeeding her child, this is definitely a high state of relaxation and meditation.

Fall in Love with Love

When we fall in love with someone, we experience life as spontaneous and—at least for a certain period of time—we are very relaxed. Why is that? It is because we are allowing love *to be* and *not trying to control the love. We are surrendered.* We are, for the most part, not thinking—and even when we are thinking, we are not clinging to the things (mental images) that we are thinking about. **And even beyond that is where the secret remains hidden in the silence. We are so in love with the object of our love that**

we have forgotten ourselves in that very love. Our minds, our thoughts, and everything else gets lost in that love. All is peaceful and still within and there are no worries. Why are there no worries? It is simply because there is no clinging and there are very few thoughts. There is one dominating thought, and that thought is selfless: "How can I please my beloved soul mate?"—and this is the source thought from which all other thoughts spring forth.

When we fall in love, we feel invincible just as we did as children—but what happens, beloved? At some point we begin to cling to the object of our love and not its source. The mind tricks us into thinking that it is the image (our beloved) outside of us that is bringing us happiness. We lose the selfless intention we initially had which brought us so much bliss. Instead of remaining a servant of love, we now begin to demand that we be served by love. This demand and selfish attitude causes us to contract and our bliss goes sour. Nature takes its course, and the external images and fleeting reflections of the world inevitably let us down. Everything that is not rooted in the eternal spiritual principles of Life will perish. **Love itself must be our first love.**

Things in the external world are *designed* to let us down. And that is because our destiny is much more profound than anything that the external world can give us. When we look at life this way, it is a lot easier to forgive. **Why would we not be willing to forgive someone whose nature was ultimately to let us down so we could grow spiritually?** The hurt caused by our unconscious search for love in the external world causes us to shift and go within thus helping us to awaken! Love is therefore still operating in its fullness and Life purpose is fulfilling itself in a most awesome way. The let down, when looked at this way, becomes such a gift. Oh Divine Love, how wonderful and adorable are your ways.

When we get emotionally attached to the object of our love and not the principle of love itself, it creates turbulence and disturbance within and we suffer. We lose that inner stillness...but do we really? We don't lose anything; we cling to the fleeting images of love and simply drop into a state of *unawareness*. The stillness of love is still there, just as the invisible air we breathe is always there even though we cannot see it. We are blinded by our own distorted eyesight, or let's say we have blocked the sunlight of awareness by creating the clouds that we spoke about earlier. The fleeting images of love changing on us are a blessing because they lead us to the Infinite unchangeable beauty within.

Remember, beloved, just like our thoughts, these images are designed to come and go. People in our lives are designed to come and go. Things are designed to come and go. Thoughts are designed to come and go. We are all, as physical forms, designed to come and go. And that is why we must become aware of the eternal formlessness of silent love from which we all emerged. Remember this, beloved friend: For someone else, you are the external world designed to let them down. The silent love that you truly are and from which all good things come is what ultimately remains.

Love, Temba Spirit

Chapter 4

The Irreplaceable Attribute of Determination

Based upon the disease-minded and stereotypical labels that society's spiritual ignorance has pre-imposed on me and many others and also themselves (such as convict, criminal, drug addict, outcast, failure, deviant, delinquent, sinner, etc.), its expectation is that I should be resentful, violent, uneducated, pissed off, and even possibly revengeful at society—yet I am none of these things. **I AM LOVE.** It is the I.D. of love that I carry in the front and back pocket of my heart. What you identify yourself with and your understanding of it is very important.

Maybe if I accepted society's description of me, I would indeed harbor hatred for a system that today has incarcerated millions of the descendants of the very people (African slaves) that built this country's economy off of their blood, sweat, and tears, yet I am not—**I am Love.**

I am aware that the very country that has incarcerated more people than any other system ever has in the history of the world was founded on some of the most horrendous crimes ever perpetuated in the history of humankind. Yet even in being aware of this, the Love in my heart for all beings is not tainted in the least bit. **I am determined to Love and Be Love!**

You see, those in the system may have labeled me a convict, but I never allowed their labels of me to penetrate deep into my consciousness. **When society said that I had descended from slaves and that my tribe was lost and untraceable, I told myself that I had descended from Divine Love and that I had come from the Ancient Tribe of Compassion!** I never let their descriptions of who they said and thought I was into my heart. The only way a concept gains power over you is if you claim it and identify with it. And just because the world calls you a duck does not mean that you have to quack, does it?

It's Not Personal

A system that was founded on murdering, stealing land, destroying culture, distorting history for selfish gain, ripping families apart, and raping Mother Earth of Her precious resources has to have been established by people who were spiritually ignorant and mentally sick. That virus of selfishness has carried on even up to this day. Just look at this world and the greed of our society. It is pitiful. What other recourse could I take but to forgive and have compassion for them? Would I not want the same from them? And is this not what so many have done for me? I even see them as God! God teaching us all what not to do and what not to be.

When *the powers that be* label people things such as convict and criminal, I realize that they are not powerful at all. They are weak-minded and spiritually insensitive; unaware themselves of who they really are. If they knew who they really were—Love—they would know who I really am—Love. What other recourse could I take but to pity them? I realize that their one or two fingers pointed at me means there are many more pointing at themselves. The negative and stereotypical labels that they have given me and many others is how they feel about themselves. It is not personal. In this awareness, **I AM FREE.**

The Heart That Breaks for All

The karma these people have to deal with is tremendous. People who are greedy and who have embodied selfishness are suffering intensely. **My heart breaks for them, just as it breaks for my brothers and sisters who suffer behind bars, and also for the rest of humanity.** You see, if I would have accepted the titles "convict" and "criminal" into the deeper regions of my being, I would be resentful, angry, revengeful, and filled with much hatred for the society that labeled me that. I would also be condemning them in my own heart and mind. Instead, I have chosen the path of understanding. Because I have chosen to identify myself with *unconditional Love,* I am free to Love the very society that judged me. I have chosen to look more deeply at why I was judged as opposed to judging that which judged me. **Oftentimes we say we do not want to be judged but then we judge that which we feel has judged us. Do your best to not get caught up in that vicious cycle of resentment and anger.**

I went through a brief phase as a teen in which I was "mad at the world," but it did not stick. **I have also had my days in which I lived a lifestyle of intense selfishness. After all, how could I speak about selfishness if I had not experienced it myself, right? This is a very important point. It helps to protect us from becoming self-righteous. We all must be determined to Love and be Love. It is very important for me not to condemn anyone in any way. Love and compassion are the cures for all the world's woes.**

At some point in my life, someone told me that I was a child of Love, of infinite Beauty, of Goodness, Forgiveness, of Solutions, and of Compassion. I allowed those benevolent thoughts into the deeper regions of my heart and mind. Those attributes made a much bigger impression on my consciousness than the ones the world tried to give me. Someone installed them into my mind and heart years before the confused and sick collective mind of the world and system got a hold of me. By the time the world's perspective entered into the layers of my surface mind, I already had a protective force field built around at least *one of the departments* of my heart's deeper levels of consciousness. A lot of the world's "thought junk" was therefore not welcomed in.

More to Be Revealed

You may be saying to yourself, "If none of the world's perspectives penetrated your deeper mental levels, what were you doing incarcerated in the first place?" Great question! At some point in my life, I must have allowed other negative thoughts to influence some of the deeper regions of my being, but it was not "the world system" that placed them into my being; it was my own parents. The unhealthy behaviors they displayed around me when I was a child had a much bigger impact on my consciousness than anything that society's confused and sick mind could have ever done. My parents' negative actions spoke much louder in my life than any of their words of goodness ever did. A child's mind is like a spiritual sponge and it absorbs everything it sees and everything it hears. My mind was no different.

From the time I was a baby up until my teenage years, I witnessed my parents using drugs and displaying other unhealthy behaviors. I allowed those unhealthy behaviors to penetrate my deeper layers of consciousness. I thought that it was okay because my parents were doing it. It appeared to me that their indulgence in drugs was bringing them happiness. I was in a lot of pain, so I wanted to experience that same happiness. They often treated me better when they were under the influence than when they were not. I let all of their "behavior junk" into my heart. There was nothing to protect me from them. It was they who were supposed to be the guardians and protectors of the deeper areas of my heart's consciousness.

By the time I realized that what my parents were doing around me was not good, I had already developed a habit. Another behavior I developed was stealing from convenience stores in order to support my habit. I was a terrible thief and would always get caught and this is why I ended up incarcerated.

The Brain that Grooves (Let's Dance!)

A literal groove had been created in my brain at that point. Society did not have to tell me that I was "an addict"—my own habit revealed that to me—but even that was a lie! I had developed addictive behaviors, but did that mean that I was a drug addict? If a person quacks like a duck, does that make him a duck? **To label a person anything other than Love is a lie!**

Before I developed addictive behavioral patterns, I was a child, was I not? Every child is Love, are they not? The "source me" is Love! The "essence me" is Love! Through the power of choice, it is up to you and me to reject all labels that have been given to us by the world or ourselves, especially if they do not testify and affirm that we are anything other than Love, Love, Love and more Love!

It is now a scientific fact that brain cells that were destroyed can be resurrected. Wow! We can create brand new brain cells! It is also a fact that any grooves that have been erected in the brain over years by negative habitual thinking and behaviors can be replaced by brand new positive ones! That means that no person who has accepted any negative labels about him or herself in the past has to *now* accept any of it! We can literally be anyone we want to be! With determination, an unshakable resolve, an optimistic attitude, a healthy and natural environment, and unstoppable effort, we can unequivocally **Reclaim Our Power!**

Any pattern of thought or action repeated many times results in a habit with a corresponding neurosignature, or brain groove. The brain is composed of approximately 100 billion cells, called neurons. A brain groove is a series of interconnected neurons that carry the thought patterns of a particular habit. Attention feeds the habit. When we give our attention to a habit, we activate the brain groove, releasing the thoughts, desires, and actions related to that habit.

The good news is that the brain is malleable. We can change our thoughts and behavior by recruiting new cells to form new brain grooves. Every thought and action is recorded within the interconnected nerve cells, and each repetition adds new depth to the brain groove. If we repeat a thought and action enough times, a habit is formed. Continued repetition strengthens the power of the habit. Inattention and lack of repetition weakens the power of the habit. These principles apply to the formation of both good and bad habits. Positive thoughts and actions create good habits. Negative thoughts and actions create harmful habits.

We can use these principles to eliminate and replace bad habits with good ones. We can gradually starve bad habits to death by not giving them our attention. As we pay more attention to forming a good habit, the new brain groove slowly gains power. Eventually, the new positive brain groove dominates the negative groove, and good habits drive out the bad. Without this transformation, spiritual growth is impossible.

—Dr. Phil Shapiro

(http://www.philipshapiro.com/art-habits.html)

Imagine me

One of my favorite songs is "Imagine Me" by the very talented gospel recording artist Kirk Franklin. At the beginning of the song you hear nothing but drums and this beautiful piano riff. With deep heartfelt gratitude and devotion, the first thing Kirk says is, "Thank you for allowing me to see myself the way you see me." Kirk Franklin is affirming that he was and is created in the Image of God, which is much more powerful to him than being created in the image of the world!

For Kirk, being created in the Image of God is to be fearfully and wonderfully made in the image of Love, eternal Beauty, and Infinite Goodness. This was the original intention for every human being. It is up to us to use our free will, also known as our power of choice, to re-align with the original intention of why we were created in the first place.

My parents therefore did me a great favor. I would not be on this awesome journey of self-discovery had they not done to me what they did. They themselves had been exposed to their parents' and the world's mental sicknesses. It is up to me now to break the cycle, by creating new brain grooves and letting the old ones return to their source, which is love. We all have the power within us to re-create ourselves and to do it with perfect success!

Garden of Eden – Consciousness

Many people look at the Garden of Eden as a place, but I look at it as also a state of awareness that we all can return to by utilizing our free will and power of determination. In the Garden of Eden (*delight* in Hebrew), Adam and Eve were originally created in the image of God (Love), yet they *chose* to create themselves in another image. Original sin was not really a sin. It was an *original choice* that was made by human beings which caused us to suffer.

This doctrine of suffering was passed on from generation to generation and it even became a part of humanity's genetic code. It became a part of humanity's collective brain groove (consciousness). Humanity's law, as opposed to Universal law, began to dominate. The doctrine that stated that we were sinners, as opposed to the divine truth that stated that we were children of Love (God), became the dominant belief and lifestyle for many. Yet that was not the original intention of Divine Love. *Original sinners*—which is another way to say *original criminals*— therefore could never be who we really are. Sinner (criminal, outcast, deviant, etc.) was a label we gave ourselves when humanity fell asleep, which in religion is known as when humanity *fell from grace.*

Society is spiritually asleep, so its labels of its people have emerged out of that same unaware state of being. Just as society gives people unhealthy and stereotypical labels (such as convicts, criminals, junkies, derelicts, and untouchables) based upon its state of spiritual sleep and mental sickness, religious people have done the same thing for thousands of years. Being asleep is a universal quality of humanity. It is never personal. Once we awaken, we will transcend all the negative labels that we have pre-imposed on each other.

When we first labeled ourselves sinners, bad, and fallen, we were actually committing the worst crime against our very own true nature.

Our forgetfulness of who we really are caused us to begin hurting ourselves by applying harmful labels to one another. Humanity did not emerge out of sin—our origin and essence nature is Love. **The human being that labels other human beings sinners and criminals is suffering profoundly. This form of suffering is so deep and subtle that they cannot see it. This is why those who declare "I AM LOVE" have great compassion for the oppressor as well as those that are being oppressed. They are never identified with being sinners or criminals; they are always great Lovers of humanity.**

We Can Enter Into the Garden of Eden—Right Here, Right Now

In humanity's collective spiritual asleepness we have given ourselves labels such as *sinner* which do not support our higher good, just as labeling people criminals, convicts, etc. does not support our collective higher good. Our true core essence nature is love, simply because Love is the source from which we *ALL* originally came. This is simple enough for a child to understand and that is why we should trust it.

When we awaken from our state of spiritual sleep, and cease to reinforce the belief that we are original sinners, we re-open *the gates* that lead back to the Garden of Eden state of consciousness. These gates are within us. Through the power of our own choice (free will) we get a chance (choice) to do it all over again. Love is eternal, so when we remember that we are that Love, we become the sons and daughters of Eternity (God). We are now ready to enter back into the garden and thus create heaven on earth.

Returning to the Garden of Eden state of consciousness takes much determination. Our power of choice has to be supported by our power of determination! We are surrounded by people who still believe they are something other than love. They have unconsciously created a negative auric energetic field that surrounds the atmosphere of Mother Earth. Even when we begin to transform, we still have to work through that negative energy. We are still connected to that energetic field, like it or not. Our determination to stay positive must be unstoppable! In the sacred scriptures, it is said that God placed Cherubim (angelic beings) at the gates of the Garden of Eden and no one was allowed back in after the *original mistake* occurred. We must put Cherubim (positive angelic energy fields) at the gates of our gardens (hearts, minds, and immediate atmosphere) and not let any negative intruders in.

If we look at the Garden of Eden as something that happened in the past, we will never get back into the Garden. If we choose to see Eden from an esoteric/spiritual perspective and an experience we can attain right now, we can re-enter, simply by choosing to do all we can to stay in the awareness of who we really are. The external reality of the Garden of Eden will then follow suit.

The only thing keeping us out of the Garden is not God, it's a choice. A choice kicked us out and a choice is what re-opens the gates all over again. It is our determination that walks us back in and it is our regular spiritual practice to eat from the Tree of Life that keeps us there.

Your Love Is Doing It

The power of determination and our regular spiritual practice is what creates a new brain groove within us. Each time one of us creates a new Garden of Eden brain groove, the energetic auric field that surrounds us and the one that surrounds Mother Earth gets purified. The heat of our spiritual practice, when filled with the power of determination and love, pushes all the negative energy to the surface of humanity's collective awareness. **It is our own positive spiritual practices that have accelerated all the negativity that we are seeing and experiencing on the planet. And that is why—in addition to utilizing the power of choice—we have to, with all of our heart's energy, exercise the power of determination!**

When we witness hatred, we have to be determined to love. When we are offended, we have to be determined to forgive. When we offend, we have to be determined to quickly offer our apology. We have to be determined not to look to be loved, but to love. We have to be determined to be the cause of benevolent causes and not the effect of negative ones.

We have to be determined to stay in the awareness that it is we who are on the spiritual path of love that are accelerating the negativity on the planet by bringing it to the surface. In understanding this, it becomes very silly to take anything personally. Like boiling water, the spiritual heat of our Love is bringing all the impurities to the surface of the pot of this world. This is an awesome awareness. When we are offended, we can laugh, knowing that it is *our own Love-energy* that is bringing the negative energy out of people.

Please remember that, beloved reader. It is very important. We are kicking all the negativity out of the Garden and out of ourselves. This is happening on the inside of us and on the outside. **Remember, Jesus came to this earth with nothing but Love and that same Love pissed a lot of people off to the point that they crucified him.** Look at all the benevolent leaders who were either jailed or murdered. Many of them were able to predict their deaths, like Martin Luther King, Jr. and Mahatma Gandhi. They knew that the spiritual heat of their love would accelerate humanity's purification, thus bringing its evils to the surface. It has to be this way.

You may wonder why there are times you can recall in which you offered your love to a situation and it seems that it made it worse. The "worse" that you think you are seeing only means that the situation was actually getting better. When someone has a bad cold and all the mucus and other stuff begins to come up, they know that healing is dawning. Your love for the situation brought some of the impurities to the surface.

So when your Love begins to push a person's negativity to the surface, know that they are being healed! Some are sicker than others so be patient, just as Life has been patient with you. **And by all means, make sure you keep your own spiritual immunity very strong, and in your patience, stay aware that you are yourself also a patient.** Love is the cure of all cures, so stay aware of this and be determined to love. That is the only thing that we can do. Remain steadfast and let your resolve be unshakable! Surround yourself with friends who are on the same spiritual path as you. This will strengthen your spiritual immunity. You must be determined to Love no matter what! The spiritual path is only for those who are courageously determined to love.

People That Offend You Are Gifts

It is very important to also remember that the people who offend you are not *original sinners* or *bad people*. They may have done some bad things, but that is not who they are at the core. They are Love. Remembering this is the greatest way you can help them and yourself. When you are around them, you will emit that love frequency and their subtle spiritual body will receive it even if they are not aware. We must do all we can to remember that they also sprang forth out of the same endless supply of love that we did. They were and are still *even now* originally created in the image of God (Divine Love).

Humility Is an Exalted State of Consciousness

We should caution ourselves to do our best to never get self-righteous. Once we become self-righteous, we are choosing to kick ourselves out of the Garden of delight. In truth, anyone who does not live in the Garden of Eden state of consciousness is a spiritual outcast. That, beloved reader, is most of humanity. That is also us if we become self-righteous.

We have to do all we can not to develop a subtle ego, for that is the hardest one to deal with. The ego that cannot be detected is ferocious. When you are on the spiritual path, it is easy to begin thinking that because "you are spiritual and a healer" and the rest of the world is not, you are better than they are. In the eyes of Love there is no such thing as "better than" or "less than." And a true healer realizes that Love is the healer that is healing all of us. A little love is the same as a lot of love in the eyes of love. Remember this, beloved reader. Humility is an exalted state of consciousness. This is very important.

Spiritual Nakedness/Innocence

Remember that in the Garden, prior to the fall, it says that Adam and Eve were naked and there was no shame associated with their nakedness. *The word naked and innocence are really synonyms.* When it says that God clothed their nakedness, it simply means that they lost their innocence. Self-righteousness is the opposite of innocence. There is nothing uglier than a person who thinks he is spiritual, but who is filled with arrogance.

In the Garden of delight (Eden), it was the serpent (snake) who expressed self-righteousness, arrogance, and pride. We who are on the spiritual path are aware that arrogance and self-righteousness are not to be found in some religious figure that is outside of us. These are characteristics that will embody us if we are not careful. When we become prideful and arrogant, we have then chosen to create ourselves in the image and likeness of a serpent, snake, devil, etc. **This can happen to all of us, and to not think it can happen to you is the first sign of it happening.**

And remember—it's all symbolic. The true essence of a snake is Love. Even the devil's truest nature is Love. After all, the scriptures say that he was once God's most beautiful angel, right? Well, I've got news for you, beloved friend; we are all still, right now, God's most beautiful angels— until we choose not to be by embracing arrogance, self-righteousness, pride, greed, lust and ego. When humanity attempts to exalt itself above the principle of Love, we fall into a state of sleep. We, through our own choices, become devils. However, when we humble ourselves to the eternal principles of compassion and selfless giving by practicing them, we stand firm and become spiritual pillars for the rest of the world. When we bow to the eternal principles, they bow to us. You see this characteristic being displayed in every true sage and true spiritual master.

When we embrace arrogance, self-righteousness, and pride, they become the false gods that suffocate our innocence and beauty. And I want to reiterate and be very clear that when I speak of *the devil*, I am not talking about the religious figure that was created by the human imagination and placed on the hot sauce bottle. I am talking about something that can potentially emerge out of the human character; we are the ones who have created our own torment (hell) and we can potentially become embodiments of selfishness if we are not careful. **Don't be alarmed; the devil only represents a school of thought and a potential part of our human character that is to be mastered and not mastered by.**

Milk is wonderful until it spoils. We must not let our spiritual milk spoil by becoming prideful. We have to use our power of determination to stay innocent and away from self-righteousness, anger, and pride. Then that very same serpent of self-righteousness loses the potency of its poison and that same poison then becomes spiritual nectar. We then gain wisdom/true serpent power and can share what we have learned with the rest of humanity. We can then begin to invite our loved ones into the

Garden of Love (Eden) where even the devil has become a dear friend and beloved one. That same serpent power that was once used for arrogance is now used to invoke the eternal power of innocence.

As I said, the devil, the serpent, etc., is just a school of thought to be mastered and not mastered by. It is really that simple. Through the power of determination, we can Reclaim our Innocence and become embodiments of Love. Once we reclaim the power of determination, anything is possible!

Love, Temba Spirit

Chapter 5

The Endless and Omnipotent Power of Forgiveness and a Bullet of Love...

I have a determined and unshakable resolve in my heart to not allow anything or anyone to make me resentful. And with the greatest intention of my heart, I now invite you into this world. In this beloved world of unconditional forgiveness, we can feed off of each others' strengths and adore each others' weaknesses. And where we once were afraid to seek forgiveness and to release its power, through our collective agreement to forgive at all cost, we will inherit fearlessness.

I also have an agreement with myself that I will not be upset about a situation for more than a few moments. I have a very radical approach to forgiveness. I have courageously aligned myself with the universal and irrevocable forgiveness contract that all awakened beings in the universe have signed with the pencils of their beloved hearts. I am grateful that grace has allowed me to be a part of that circle: **"If someone tried to kill me and I lived, even then I would forgive!"** This, beloved, is my all-powerful forgiveness mantra. In fact, when I was a teenager, I was shot in the chest and almost murdered by someone who was in a rival street gang. No, I am not still in a gang; I renounced my gang affiliation (on national television) years ago. However, I remember what I am about to tell you as if it were yesterday. I would love to share this true story with you.

The Bullet of Love That Saved My Life

A few days after I came home from the hospital from being shot, I was told that the person who shot me was across the street and that we could now take our revenge. "Ant is across the street, we can get him," is what one of my gang buddies said. I looked across the street and, lo and behold, there was Anthony, standing outside the store, just as I had been informed he was. Right then a gentle yet powerful voice within the depths of my being spoke to me and said, **"Go across the street, look him in his eyes, and tell him that you forgive him."** It is hard to really explain it. It's not like there was an actual audible voice, however in the silence of my heart, this was the message that silent Love conveyed to me.

That silent inaudible voice was the universal consciousness of love, the Christ Consciousness if you will, the good within, that could not and would not kill another human being. Even still, my palms were sweaty and my heart was beating rapidly from nervousness. Remember, I had just been shot by this guy and I was fresh out the hospital with a collapsed lung, a bullet lodged in my chest and not a lot of physical strength. By that time in my life I had lost at least 30 friends to brutal murder. My neighborhood was like a war zone. Thank God we did not have access to more advanced weapons.

Grace

Everything about the gang culture I was in said to kill him—but something beautiful at the core of my being had spontaneously emerged from the depths of my essence and had commanded me to do something else. How I was able to do this is a great mystery to me to this day. The truest word that I can apply to what happened through me that day is God's beloved Grace. I know us transformational and new age folks do not like to use words like faith, grace and God; Oh well, that is real for me.

Because...somehow, some way, I mustered up the courage, walked across the street and said, "Ant, I forgive you. Now get out of here because they plan on killing you!" In that moment, I had reclaimed my power! My power to Love. The fear was there, but I knew that I had the ability to stop the vicious cycle of bloodshed simply by choosing to forgive him. That subtle intuition was grace. I was aware that I did not want to kill another human being. In those precious moments, saving a life became more important to me than taking revenge. My heart did not want to kill him or hurt him. I survived my bullet wound so that I could forgive! We are all here to give-for (for-give) the sake of Love. I know that this **New Testament of Temba Spirit** is only one amongst the many of humanity's inspirational stories of forgiveness.

And I also want you to realize that I still went on to get into much more trouble after this experience. The point is this: In spite of all the tragedy and mishap that occurred throughout my life, somewhere underneath and also above it all, was the presence of innate goodness. And this is what we all must remember about ourselves and others. The capacity to forgive absolutely everyone and everything exists within us all. Please absolutely never forget this!

Uncompromising Forgiveness

There are law-abiding citizens in society who are not willing to forgive the simplest things —and here I was a so-called juvenile delinquent who was willing to forgive the person who tried to kill me. In other words, don't judge a book by its cover. Love is present inside every Book of Life, even if the cover is extremely damaged—but how many will open it up to courageously search to find that Love? **Always look for the good, the love,** and the beauty in every situation and they will be made known to you. Remember that every pile of dung can be converted into the sweetest-smelling incense. This happens in India every day.

By society's and the gang's standards, I was supposed to take my revenge and kill Anthony. However, by the standards of Love, I was supposed to forgive him and thus one day (right now), give others the courage and inspiration to forgive through this example. I had to get shot so I could experience Love in this profound way and therefore contribute to the acceleration of humanity's spiritual evolution. This is what the energy of forgiveness does.

The great shift that is occurring on this planet is occurring everywhere and in every "hood" throughout the boundless universe, not just in certain spiritual circles. For Consciousness to truly be universal and omnipresent (everywhere) it has to be happening this way. In forgiving Anthony then, I was collaborating with all conscious beings on the planet that uncompromisingly declare that, **"We will forgive come hell or high water!"** I was participating in setting the tone for a new paradigm to come in then and even right now. Would you have ever thought or imagined that you would be learning about the power of forgiveness from a former gang member and ex-convict? **The same thing occurred two thousand years ago when a convicted felon who was at his final stage of death row uttered the most powerful words, "Forgive them Father for they know not what they do."** You all remember our beloved brother Jesus, don't you? This ushered in the new cycle and this energy of Divine Love bumped me on the head and dropped down into my heart right smack on the west side slums of Chicago 2,000 years later. **<u>Uncompromising forgiveness is a legacy that everyone on the spiritual path must be determined to carry on.</u>**

Divine beings come into this realm to bring in the new cycles and paradigms. And I've got news for you, beloved friend, you are one of those chosen Divine beings and counted as a part of the great and universal circle of compassion and forgiveness! Universal consciousness loves to use stories like mine and others like it for shock value because they grab humanity's attention. People have little or no choice but to open up to the possibility of forgiveness working in and through their lives when someone reveals to them that they forgave the person who literally tried to kill them. These extreme and most needed experiences of forgiveness are a way that Life is saying to humanity, **"You are wasting time. Wake up! Be courageous, forgive, and free yourself!"**

When I tell you that I would even forgive a person who tried to kill me, I am not just trying to sound profound. This is my direct experience. I forgave the person who shot me and stopped a potential war. This experience revealed to me that there is a profound spiritual power that dwells within all of us. **To this day, I still live with the bullet lodged in my chest—just a couple of inches away from my heart. Oh how fortunate I am.**

What a great gift it was for me to get shot! That gun and that bullet, and that angry and hurting person who shot me helped me to experience God and to glimpse greater spiritual potential! **By a couple of inches the bullet missed my heart—and I believe to this day that's why I am so close to Love. The same bullet that barely**

missed my heart woke up the power of my heart! I needed to go through a situation that deep and intense so that my character could develop spiritual depth. I could have just left the scene, went home, and forgiven Anthony in my heart. But I had to face him so that I could spiritually evolve and guide others to do the same. In order to evolve spiritually we must embrace inner courage and forgive absolutely everything! And sometimes this happens in unexplainable spontaneous ways, and that is called Grace.

And yes, as I said, beloved friend, there was fear present when the voice told me to forgive him, and it even became more turbulent when this same voice said to walk up to him and tell him that. Yet there was also inner courage present —and that spiritual courage is what came out victorious! Here's what I am hoping millions of people will contemplate after reading this: **"If**

Temba's Spirit could forgive the person who tried to kill him two weeks after it happened, I can forgive the person who has offended me right now." I am hoping to inspire that type of spiritual depth and courage. I sincerely want you to be free.

Even as a gang member I was a light worker. I did not realize this then—but now, as my spiritual awareness has matured, that day I got shot and that day I chose to forgive has become much more profound and beautiful and also so spiritually relevant to this day and this current time.

This also lets me know that we walk by light workers every day and do not notice them. My life represents every human being alive that has been under-estimated by the world and even by themselves. **I am the potential spiritual**

fertilizer that is contained inside of every pile of sh••. Most people look at a pile of crap and will write it off as purposeless; however, the true spiritual aspirant will sniff that same pile of crap until they are able to smell it as a sweet bed of flowers, knowing that it too has a great Life purpose. A light worker therefore does not deny the darkness. On the contrary, they see all darkness as a womb or a place for something brand new, precious and beautiful to be birthed through. The key is to realize that each and every last one of us has the potential to be Light Workers. And I've got more news for you: That person who the world has written off as useless (a pile of crap) will be used by Life to bring the Kingdom of Light (awareness) to this earth in a most profound way.

How grateful I am that it was me Anthony shot that day. Who knows? Maybe if it had been someone else, that person might not have had the courage to forgive and his fear may have led him to kill Anthony. This would have in turn caused others to want to kill. And like Gandhi said, **"An eye for an eye leaves the whole world blind."** Maybe I would have lost 60 childhood friends to brutal murder as opposed to the 30, had it been someone else who Anthony shot. In seeing it this way, we can all take it as a great gift and honor when someone offends us, knowing that Life has entrusted us to Love humanity with no conditions.

You are not just freeing yourself when you forgive; You are helping to free all beings

Forgiveness is just that powerful! When we forgive we are participating in the practice of unconditional love. In exercising its power, we are literally helping the aura of the planet to transform and potentially saving lives. Please never believe that you are only helping yourself when you forgive. Consciousness does not work that way. One droplet of forgiveness causes a ripple of love to occur throughout all creation. This is what Christ-Consciousness is all about.

Forgiveness is a much deeper spiritual power than we think. When our beloved brother Jesus/Yashua forgave humanity 2,000-plus years ago, it carved an eternal and spiritual imprint into the awareness of humanity's collective consciousness. Every time you forgive you are doing the same exact thing. Please accept this with all your heart. When you exercise the eternal principle of forgiveness, you become just that powerful.

Love, Temba Spirit

Chapter 6

The Dynamic Power of Conscious Choice

I am bless-fully counted amongst the millions that have been through just about every kind of human suffering that can be experienced in this modern-day world. I have been through addictions, child abuse, and all sorts of violence, incarceration, racism, depression, hunger, homelessness, low self-esteem, and unhealthy relationships—yet **I AM STILL HERE**! I have been through multiple near-death experiences, including jumping out of a second story building (landing on my knees and then flat on my face), overdosing on drugs, being almost beaten to death, and getting shot in the chest, lung collapsing, etc.—**yet I AM STILL HERE!**

Let's All Dance the Sacred Dance of Life

Through it all, absolutely none of it had the power to destroy me. We are all still here, beloved friend. If you have been through all the hell that I have (and you probably have—maybe even worse) we both have something to celebrate! Through it all, none of it had the power to keep me from forgiving. Through it all, none of it had the power to keep me from forgiving myself. Through it all, none of it had the power to keep me resentful. Through it all, none of it had the power to keep me (for more than a short period of time) from embracing and seeing the good. Through it all, none of it had the power to keep me from being willing to give the person less fortunate than I the shirt off of my back. Through it all, none of it had the power to make me not smile, laugh, or inspire those around me. Through it all, none of it had the power to keep me from believing in the power of my own heart. Through it all, none of it had the power to make me not love.

I am dancing the sacred dance of victory and if you take a moment and consider all the sh•• you have gone through, you might begin dancing ecstatically with me. The details of our lives may be different on the surface, but deep down, beloved friend, our pain is the same—so by all means, let's dance! The way we dance the dance of Life is to do our best to enjoy each moment and live like the celebrities that we all are. No! I do not mean actors. **The new paradigm definition of a celebrity is someone who "Celebrates Life!"**

Now, Let's Dance On...

I am a walking miracle! Not because of anything I have done, but because of what the Perfect Spiritual Power that dwells in me has done in me, through me, and around me— *in spite of me!* **We are all walking miracles. Life itself is a miracle!** But what really blows my mind the most, is that nothing I have gone through had the power to stop me from sincerely caring for everyone. My heart earnestly wants all beings to attain their highest good and experience it perpetually. **I believe that deep down underneath all the funk of life, we all sincerely want supreme happiness to be attained by everyone.**

After going through all the hell and coming out on the other side with a heart unscathed, what other choice do I have but to accept and embrace that there is a power within us all that is greater than any of life's challenges and hardships? This eternal power in us is greater than and beyond us, yet it is US! Mind-boggling isn't it? **Yet through it all, WE ARE STILL HERE!** I am not glorifying *myself or us* in any way, yet this is a very glorious Life that we are all participating in. I am most definitely exalting to the utmost this sublime, omnipotent, and infinitely profound, yet extraordinarily simple supreme Power of Love that I simply refer to as **THE HEART**. You may ask, "All that just to describe the heart?" Absolutely! **All that just to describe your heart. Your heart is that important to me. In fact, because I view the heart as the source of Life, I came from you and you came from me. Your Love is my essence and mine is yours. We are one in that Love…Are you dancing yet?**

One Similar Thread

I cannot speak of your actual experiences for you; I would not dare violate the sacredness of your scripture in that way. However, I can say that if you have lived in this day and age, you have gone through hell! We human beings have created much hell on our beloved planet earth. The **Christians** confirm this when they pray, **"Thy Kingdom come, Thy will be done."** They are praying for more heaven to come down to earth because they are going through hell! **Muslims** say, **"Assalamu Alaikum, Peace be upon you."**—yet look at all the warfare in many of the Islamic regions. War creates hell! More of us should declare, **"Peace be upon you!"** Our world is starving for peace right now.

People of the **Judaic Faith** say **"Shalom."** They want more peace as well. And can you blame them? Look at all the hell in Israel. The **Buddhist** meditates, expresses compassion, and speaks of an abode within referred to as *Nirvana*, which describes a state of being that is free from suffering. Buddhists put great emphasis on doing all they can to support all beings in becoming free from suffering. Even the **Dalai Lama** had to flee his own country because of all the hell on earth that was created for the **Tibetan people**. This only confirms that our world is filled with much suffering. Suffering and hell are synonyms, right?

Hindus greet each other by saying **Namaste**, which means **"I bow to the Consciousness** (Divine Being-ness) within you." India has millions of starving people and also 250,000,000 people who have been labeled dalits ("untouchables") by the spiritually sick caste system. That's a lot of people being tormented in hell. I think you get the point.

Every spiritual way of life that I just mentioned above uses the power of words in an attempt to invoke the possibility of bringing more heaven into humanity's sphere of existence. In speaking these beautiful thoughts into existence and collectively doing all we can to help this world become a more heavenly home for the planet earth's children, we are indeed affirming that this world is filled with much hell.

However...

The Hell We Have Created Is Waking Us Up!

We have all gone through hell—and not only that, we have also created it! And even now, there is still so much good that is present. Because we are hell's creator, we are also its destroyer! So therefore, I may not know the exact details of what you have gone through personally, however, based upon the current over-all hellish conditions on this planet, we both know good and damn well that we have all definitely experienced a lot of hell! Yet, beloved friend, through it all—**you ARE STILL HERE!** There is indeed a Power in you, through you, and around you that is greater than all of it.

When I speak of hell, I am talking about the one we experience right here, not the religious one, though I have used religious examples to make a point. I cannot speak about the religious hell that some believe comes after death because I have never experienced it. And why would I waste my precious spiritual power on believing in such a dreadful abode, especially when I could use that same energy to make this world a better place right here, right now? **Is there not enough dread right here to deal with?**

When I speak of hell I am referring to the hell of greed, poverty, corruption, war, starvation, anger, deceit, ego, and all other things created by humanity's collective selfishness. The divine paradox is this: **The very same hell that we have created is also helping us all to awaken. Our own collective selfishness has created so much hell on our beloved planet that it is forcing us to embrace the principle of selfless Love.** Life is benevolently giving us a needed break from the very hell that we ourselves have created. The universal consciousness within us is breaking down the old paradigm walls of hell! This is happening in, to, and through us whether we are consciously on the spiritual path or not. **Anyone who is tired of the hellish conditions that exist in this world is actually in just being fed up, making room for a new and heavenly reality to manifest in and through their lives.**

Heaven Is a Much Healthier Choice

Good can be found in everything if we look for it. But if we do not consciously search for it, the mind will lie to us and tell us that there is none there. That is why many people continue to create hell. They believe that there is nothing but negativity present based upon what they "think" they are seeing when they look out into the world. **Therefore the search for Heaven has to begin within your own being. If we do not find it there (within), we will not find it anywhere. Once we find it within, we will begin to see heaven even in the areas of life in which it appears that there is none.**

There are some who say that there is no heaven "way out there" somewhere. I would not say that, for I believe that love is omnipresent (everywhere) and that love is indeed ever-expanding heavenly existence. **But what I can say is this: Even if we make it to heaven "out there" someday but don't have heaven within us when we get there, (wherever there is) we will just create another hell all over again.** Whereever we go we take ourselves with us, correct? We might as well create heaven right here, right now! The same power within us that has enabled us to create hell on earth is the same power that can also enable us to create more heaven. We all hold this power of choice in the palm of our hands and the center of our hearts, do we not? With this power of choice we can use the fire of Life to warm a house, or to burn it down. The eternal flame of choice is there within us all. It is simply how we decide to use it that makes the difference.

To even realize that we have the power to choose is a great attainment. We all have made choices throughout our lives, have we not? It is when we begin to *decide* to make choices that we are waking up. When we begin to awaken to the reality that it is we who have the choice to either create heaven or hell, we are reclaiming our spiritual power to choose and creating and assuring a prosperous and promising destiny!

The Divine Ego

Spiritual Power is most definitely not like worldly Power. Worldly power is based upon ego and being in control of the world or of somebody else. Spiritual power is based upon Divine Love and being in control of yourself and surrendered to the principles of a greater good. Divine Love is the one thing that emanates in and through all things and also unifies all things. Ego is the one thing that *appears* to emanate in all things and also *appears* to separate all things. However, in truth we are never really separated from anything. The ego is therefore an illusion and doesn't really emanate anywhere! But it is a *real illusion* so we have to deal with it. If we don't, it deals with us.

Here is a good rule of thumb to help us know whether or not we are living a life filled with ego, or a life filled with love: When you feel separate, alone, isolated, or confined, you know you are in a state of ego. On the other hand, when you feel alive, unified, and in your heart, you know that you are in a state of love and aligned with the Divine Ego. This state of being has nothing to do with your outer circumstances, though your outer circumstances can complement it. It is more an experience of your heart than anything else. I have been in a prison cell isolated and away from the rest of the world, yet had the most fortunate experience of oneness with everything. On the other hand, I have been physically free in the world and felt separated from everything.

You Are Never Alone

When I was in that prison cell, it became the Heart of Divine Love/God/Consciousness. For months through the unexplainable power of Grace, I cried tears of compassion on behalf of the suffering world. I realized that there were so many more that had it far worse than I and this broke my heart into pieces of compassion. I realize now that if one person suffers, a part of all of us suffers. Not just a part of all of us, but a part of everything in creation. When I cried tears for the suffering world, my experience was that everything in creation was crying with me and through me. I would ball up on my steel prison bunk and say, "Amma (Love) take it all away (the things of the world), but please never take away the gift of being able to serve."

Whenever you are hurting, remember that a part of everything in creation is hurting with you. In seeing it this way, you become one with the whole of creation and your hurt and pain will be transformed into great blissful waves of spiritual power. Please remember that you are a part and parcel of a whole universe. **Whenever you are crying, creation is also crying with you and through you.** And whenever you are dancing, smiling and celebrating, just know that the entire universe is dancing, smiling and celebrating with you as well. **This is true universal consciousness.** We are truly never alone. The next time you shed a tear please remember this.

Through those tears of compassion, I became one with everything in creation. This was my direct experience. The power of Grace within me, through me and around me took me beyond my power to choose. I had no choice but to cry. I could not help it. The ocean of Love poured through me on its own accord. I was not choosing it. Divine Love's tears chose to make their home in my heart. I had tapped into the endless ocean of forgiveness and compassion. I cried this way every day for months. **The prison cell was no longer a prison cell, it had become the beloved heart of God**. This is why I say that my experience was that creation was crying with and through me. There was an infinitely profound "something" within me that sucked my power to choose right into its eternal vacuum. After that my power to choose was transcended. That 'something' (that I choose to call love) made a choice to choose to adore me so profoundly that my **"free will"** for those precious moments was absorbed.

I did not become a saint. I became aware of the saint that dwell-ed within all beings. I did not become anything special or greater than. I became so little, so vulnerable and so helpless. I will forever remain one of the Universal Mother's little lost children, Temba Spirit; And there is no greater gift than to be lost in Her Love.

I would be lying to you if I told you that I have some type of perfect spiritual formula to help you experience the internal state of loving everyone. I have to bring myself back into this awareness all the time. I just know that even in my forgetfulness, deep down there will always be a presence of Infinite Love that truly and eternally adores all beings. **I call this presence Amma, but in whatever form Love appears and reflects through and to your consciousness, Temba's Spirit will adore it.** I am now even lost for words in trying to intellectually describe what it all really means. I can say that it is a sacred Love affair that happens in the deepest depths of your very own being. Even if you display human emotions on the surface and go through life's typical challenges and even if you struggle with certain issues, there is something deep within the depths of your soul that knows that you will always have a deep, sincere, and genuine love for everyone. **This deep sincere Love that my heart has for all beings is the presence of the Universal Mother within.** In the sacred place of my very own heart, all beings will always have a place to live. In my heart no one will ever be homeless, lost, orphaned or forgotten. I long for this reality to be perpetually experienced by all.

A Spiritual Guarantee

I will be the first to admit that embracing innocence, remaining teachable, and doing all you can to keep your heart open are the only true techniques that I can recommend based upon what this bless-ed Life has taught me. Throughout this book, I have jokingly made spiritual guarantees to you—but in truth and in the integrity of raw honesty, I cannot guarantee anything. I know that there are many books out there that make guarantees and promises to the reader. But truthfully, no book writer can guarantee you a true spiritual experience simply by telling you to read his or her book. We have to put what we read into practice.

This is Super Important

Your willingness to practice is the only way you can guarantee your spiritual success. You can read about a piece of fruit as much as you want and you will never taste it. Until you eat it you will never truly experience the benefits of the fruit. It is the same with spiritual food. You can only taste and enjoy the Spirit by Spiritual practice. So the guarantee is coming from you, not the book you are reading or the writer who wrote it. It is all coming from your decision to put what you have learned into practice. Any true Spiritual Master will tell you this. Once you put what you are reading into practice you will attain spiritual experience. Once this happens you will go to read spiritual books and realize, "I experienced that; I know what they are talking about." For many of us that is already happening. And this is only the beginning.

Life Chose Us—Now Let's Choose Life!

True Spiritual Power gives us the choice to choose it, just as air gives us the choice to breathe it. Air does not need you. You need air. Spiritual Power does not need us. It is we who have to reclaim our spiritual Power. The Spiritual Power does not have to reclaim anything, correct?

So, on that note, let's take a moment and breathe in deep and exhale deep. In taking that conscious deep breath, we all just chose Life, did we not? Actually, we do this every time we inhale the beloved breath of Life. We just have to learn to breathe consciously. **True spiritual power descends on us when we give our power to choose over to the Spiritual Power that sustains all Life, just like we do when we breathe. Every time we breathe we are surrendering to Love and "Thy Will is Being Done in us, through us and all around us."**

Something beyond our human com-prehension gave us all the power to choose Life? What is it? Do we honestly know and more importantly do we have to!" That simple contemplation will help us to become open. In that contemplation is where we come to realize that some questions just cannot be answered and don't have to be either. The answer to this question is beyond intellectual comprehension, so we have therefore described it as the Great Mystery, The first Cause, The Source, The Supreme Energy of Good, Universal Consciousness, The Creator, Divine Love—and another title humanity has come up with in an attempt to explain the unexplainable is God—Who has also been known historically as the servant of all servants. Love,Temba Spirit

Chapter 7

The Eternal Legacy of a Servant

All titles—such as reverend, minister, pastor, swami, guru, saint, rabbi, priest, imam, chief, king, queen, shaman, friend, God, and even human being—are all really describing one title and that is **servant**. The title of servant is the highest spiritual position in the universe that we can attain and that it why it is said that God (who is Love) is the servant of all servants.

You probably noticed that I included the title "human-being" in my auspicious collection of titles. For some of us it may seem far beyond our spiritual reach to become a rabbi, priest, or guru; however, we can all relate to being human. Oftentimes when we think about what being human is we minimize it by saying things like, "I am only human." Or, alternately, we feed our egos by claiming to be the only beings on the earth that have the ability to express intelligence and reason.

How can we look out at all the chaos happening on the earth and honestly continue to declare that we are the only intelligent beings on this beloved earth? We have literally placed the concept of "intelligence" in the box of our collective human ego. Our ability to "think" is the main thing that we believe sets us apart from the rest of the animal kingdom. And that is the problem! We have set ourselves apart from the animals, which sets us apart from nature, which sets us apart from using true intelligence and being aligned with Divine Intelligence (which is really just common sense).

A Closer Look at True Intelligence

Mother Nature and the animals use common sense. When nature says it's time to go, the animals leave! But what do we supposedly *intelligent humans* do? We build houses on areas that are known to have regular earthquakes and landslides. That's real intelligent! The animals' intelligence says, "We cannot conquer Mother Nature; we better listen to her and move on." We call that instinct—but could it be that it is really true intellect? Saying animals use their instincts is just another way of saying they are more sensitive to the voice of the Divine than we humans are. Animals know what to do and where to go when the sh** hits the fan. *They* are the intelligent ones.

Consider this introduction to the PBS show NATURE:

An elephant trumpets wildly, breaks a chain holding it to a

tree, and flees to higher ground — just before a massive tsunami crashes ashore, drowning hundreds of thousands of people.

Did the elephant know the deadly wave was coming?

That's the question explored by NATURE's "Can Animals Predict Disaster?"

In interviews with scientists and eyewitnesses, NATURE probes the evidence that some animals may have senses that allow them to predict impending natural disasters long before we can.

Some creatures, for instance, may be able to "hear" infrasound—

sounds produced by natural phenomena, including earth-quakes, volcanoes, and storms, that are inaudible to the human ear. This ability may give elephants and other animals enough time to react and flee to safety.

Another explanation may lie in animals' sensitivities to electro-magnetic field variations. Quantum geophysicist Motoji Ikeya has found that certain animals react to changes in electrical currents. He now regularly monitors a catfish, the most sensitive of the creatures he has tested, to aid him in warning others of coming disaster.

Follow NATURE as it reexamines ancient ideas about how animals can predict disaster which are now gaining credence in scientific circles.

(http://www.pbs.org/wnet/nature/ episodes/can-animals-predict-disaster/introduction/130/)

The Sacred Blood of the Earth

The human being's intelligence says, "We are in charge, let's conquer nature." What is the end result of human beings' so-called intelligence? Just ask all the geese, fish, and all the human beings on the coast that were affected by the BP oil spill in 2010. Just ask the ocean. You see, it was certain people's so called *intelligence* that told them to begin digging for oil in the first place.

The animals and all the indigenous people on the planet know that the oil is Mother Earth's blood. When we take her blood (oil) for selfish gain, it is just like a vampire sucking the blood of his victim. When we see a vampire biting someone's neck and drinking someone's blood on TV it repulses us because we imagine it happening to us. Should we not be repulsed when we see cooperate vampires biting on the neck of our beloved Mother Earth hoping to suck her resources dry?

Look at the way a person is depicted after a vampire has sucked all the blood out of his or her body; the person looks sickly pale and dead-like. We get closer to this reality happening to our beloved Mother Earth every time we take something from her bosom that should have been left alone. Going on these collective human ego trips about how intelligent we are and buying into this idea that we are more, most, and the only intelligent beings on this planet has helped our beloved planet to become really messed up.

True Wealth

Many of our hearts have become dry like deserts as a result of our self-centered approach and total misunderstanding as to what true wealth really is. Mother Nature is our true wealth! The air we breathe is priceless wealth! **You cannot breathe money in any of its many forms, can you? If you value your money over oxygen you are insane! That is just plain ole' crazy. The water we drink is priceless wealth! You cannot drink your money either, can you? The** trees and plants that create our oxygen are priceless wealth! Human life is priceless wealth! When we return to this understanding, we are waking up, and then and only then are we exercising true intelligence.

Looking for satisfaction in the external world by means of trying to conquer Nature has been one of the key elements that have enabled this spiritually dry desert-like existence of humanity to unfold. Being the takers of nature's resources as opposed to the givers of our nature's greatest resource, Love, has backfired on us over and over again. **Spiritual moisture and Love's lubrication will come to us swiftly when we decide to become servants again**. We look to be served by life rather than being the servants of life and this is where our problems begin. We lose the awareness that being human in and of itself is a gift from life and that simply being alive is proof that we are already being served.

Instead of looking to be served by life, we but need to become more aware of how wonderful life has been to us. Once we realize how blessed we are, becoming a servant as a way to say thank you to life for all that it has given us will be effortless. Above, I mentioned God as being described as the servant of servants; God is just another way to describe Life itself. Life itself is the servant of all servants and it was from out of this great legacy of spiritual brilliance, that we have all emerged.

A Few Specific Ways That Life Is Already Serving Us

Let's take a look at a few of the wonderful ways in which life is already serving us. We can start with the air that we breathe. We did not

231

create air, did we? Air is serving us. We are not serving it. Without air there is no life, at least not for us. We need air. Air does not need us. Next there are plants, trees, animals, and water, which are just a few of the benevolent ways that life sustains our lives. Let's not forget the gravitational pull on the planet and the electromagnetism that allows us to be grounded on the earth and not be hurled out into space in the form of atoms.

And then there is your heartbeat, the blood that circulates throughout your body, and your nerves that send messages to your brain from different parts of your body and allow you to feel. What about your eyes? They allow you to see. And what about your ears that allow you to hear, and your hands that allow you to touch? What about the legs and feet that allow us to stand, walk, and run? These are all ways in which life is benevolently serving us.

What about the earth's soil that allows us to grow vegetables? What about the vegetables that provides protein and nutrients? All of the beautiful things I mentioned above are descriptions of various forms of life that are all working together in a delicate universal balance that is serving us. They do not need us. We need them! This should humble us.

Let's Pause to Breathe and Say Thank You

Now stop for a moment and take a deep breath. Next, silently within your heart, tell life "Thank you for serving me all these years." Many of us have never done this. We have even been disturbed when people have not thanked us—yet we have neglected to thank the very breath of life that sustains us. It's really time to Reclaim our Power! Make a spiritual commitment with your heart right now that you will do much more to remember to regularly thank life for blessing you with its presence.

One of the greatest ways in which this can be done is to first embrace the attitude of a servant. Once you allow this new energy called *Life-gratitude* to saturate your mind by contemplating it consistently, the spiritual energy created from your servant attitude will embody you. A true life of fulfillment can only come after we become servants. **Just ask Jesus, Buddha, Krishna, or any of their Mothers! Without their Mothers serving them by giving birth to them, breast-feeding them and raising them, there would have been no them!**

Everything in creation is serving us so that we can be us. When we become servants, we align ourselves with the supportive energy of Mother Nature and also of the entire universe! This is not a philosophy. This is an exact spiritual science. The great Master Teacher Jesus himself once said, "The son of humanity did not come to be served but to serve." The reason all spiritual masters who have walked this earth have always had the greatest of life's support in carrying out their divine assignments is simply because they embraced the attitude of a servant. **They were determined to love and to serve.**

Love, Temba Spirit

Chapter 8

8 Good Questions

1) *Temba, throughout the book you keep coming back to the metaphor of being like a child. What were you like as a child? As a child, did you feel a connection with an underlying presence of love? If so, do you remember what it felt like the moment when you "lost" or "forgot" it?*

There isn't really a "what it was like then" to speak about. My experience now is that of a child. It is just that the child who I am now remembers the child that I was then— I'm the same child, just with a more expanded awareness. It's the same child, on the same journey, in the same Life. We are all just expanded versions of the same innocence, love, and beauty that we were then and still are even now. I do not remember a time when I was not that child. I have always been myself. The "then child" doesn't really exist. Now is Reality. We are all, right now, the same child within simply with more awareness of who we really are.

Once the awareness of love is resurrected into your consciousness, it's as if it was never lost in the first place, because it never really was. It just *felt* or *seemed* like it was lost. Once your awareness of "what really is" resurrects, you contemplate the entire journey, no matter how painful it may have been, as a journey of love that occurred within your very own being. The forgetfulness was a needed part of the journey that leads you to awakening, remembering, and reclaiming. Your entire Life's experiences are then realized and perceived to be priceless. Both the states of being "asleep" and being "awake" are

Life's precious gifts and lessons. Please contemplate this deeply.

Love is never lost. We just have to awaken to its awareness. When we are asleep, reality on the other side of sleep still exists; we just are not aware of it. We are still breathing air on this side of reality when we are dreaming and at the same time breathing air in the dream world. Yet in the dream world, we are not aware that we are breathing air on the other side of Life. **We are breathing a form of air in two different dimensions at the same time in order to simultaneously exist in both worlds. This is proof that multiverses do exist. Wow! How wonderful awareness is.**

When we awaken to one degree of awareness, there is always another degree above it to awaken to. This should humble us and also give us a reason to celebrate this beloved and awesome journey of life. This also makes life fun and childlike. This is true spiritual adventure. The reality of Life and Love is present in every dimension and we should do our best to remember this. This takes the faith and trust of innocence to accept. And once we experience what we believe in, then and only then do we truly acquire true spiritual knowledge, wisdom, and understanding.

The sacred energetic presence of a child pervades every dimension of Life because the child is indeed Pure Consciousness. The child knows everything good because he or she believes and trusts in everything good. At the same time the child remains empty and knows nothing because he or she remains open to all things new. The reason why children are able to see into other dimensions is because their innocence has the ability to invoke the presence of beings that those with egos cannot. A child's innocence is so awesomely compelling that it can literally attract and pull beings out of other dimensions at will. **Animals are imbued with this same quality of Innocence and can also see into other realms and communicate with beings in the subtle dimensions of Life.** A child does not have an ego to block the flow of communication with other life forms. Children don't have egos simply because they do not perceive them. The concept of an ego is insignificant and meaningless to a child. This is an instance when unawareness becomes a blessing. Animals also do not have egos, because the ego is a man-made *adult* concept. Adults created the concept of ego and thus have pre-imposed it and projected it on to others **just as I am doing right now to make the point**. Ego cannot exist in a heart that is innocent.

The ego-less one is also known as the sacred child. This is why Jesus said, "Unless ye become like a child- you could not enter into the realm of heaven." Heaven is simply the realm in which all possibilities exist. Children live in a state of heaven. The inner child is not *just* some hurting creature that needs to be healed. The inner child is God! A child can make a stuffed animal come alive simply because the stuffed animal is alive inside the divine mind of a child! The child sees into the essence of all life and appears to create life where there isn't any. But really, it is just that the child's mind has not been tainted by the doubts and strange beliefs of this adult-ego orientated world. **And a mind that has not been corrupted or tainted by the silly beliefs of the world is a mind that is pervaded with God-Consciousness, which is also known as the realm of all-possibilities.**

Love is always present, sustaining us in perfect benevolence. Life itself is Love's presence within us, through us and around us, as us, ever unfolding into greater degrees of Innocence and Beauty. Even the person that has a tendency to complain about Life is being blessed by Life to be able to complain in the first place. In every realm of existence Life is always rooting for us.

You also mentioned something about feeling Love all the time.

Please allow me to humbly address this. I experience the presence of love very often (including every time I breathe air), but I do not like to limit Love to just being a "feeling" because feelings fluctuate and are fleeting. They come in and out just like everything else in the temporal external world. I keep the concept and my experience of what I believe Love is very simple.

Love is the air we breathe and the sunshine, which is constant. The air we breathe has never let us down, has it? That has nothing to do with feelings. The air that sustains us is also known as the Breath of Life. I experience Love in every moment not because of some "airy-fairy" spiritual concept or because I am enlightened. Who knows if I am enlightened or not? I am not attached to that concept. I experience Love in each moment because of how and what I perceive Love to be. Love is absolutely everything that is enabling me to experience Life. And that is regardless of if it feels good to me or not. In this way, Love has become very simple.

Love can, however, move through our feelings similar to how sound waves can travel through water. When the sound of love travels through us, it transmutes into intense feelings of compassion and joy. The sound of Love is an inner calling that moves us into action when we see someone hurting. And it is equally what happens inside of us when we see someone happy and a great surge of celebratory energy runs through us. When this happens we are compelled to dance the beloved dance of eternity.

2) *Another theme you continually return to is that of motherhood and the maternal. Why do you think this concept is so significant for you?*

As soon as we say baby, child, innocence, etc., the mother and father principles are both invoked. There is no child without parents. This is a super-natural law. The reason we place so much emphasis on the maternal side of things is because the Mother/Maternal represents an undying compassion for her children. If we look out at this world and see what we are lacking, it is compassion. Those who are aligned with compassion are aligned with the Universal Mother. Those who are aligned with the Universal Mother are aligned with compassion. It's just that simple.

Even when the Bible speaks of a New Jerusalem coming down out of heaven as a Bride adorned for Her Husband, it is talking about the return of the Sacred Mother/Compassion. Fifty years ago it was unheard of to even speak about women preaching in churches, but now in this great day of awakening and maternal cycle of Life, female preachers and teachers are popping up everywhere and being honored and adored by men. The Divine Mother as a Universal principle has to be exalted in this day and time to restore the supreme balance of Life. Both the wings of the feminine and masculine must flap in order for the bird of humanity to fly successfully. Compassion must begin to reign supreme.

The Universal Mother must re-awaken within us all. The reason why I place so much emphasis on the Maternal is simply because she has graciously awakened in me. I am a Mother in a man's body. The quality of innocence and the principle of the Universal Mother go hand in hand. You cannot have one without the other.

3) *You've talked about how suffering can be the driving force behind transformation. Why do you think that is? And is there anything we can do to be more aware or receptive so that we don't require AS MUCH suffering before we awaken or reconnect with spirit?*

Those are both good questions. To not want to suffer any more is an awakened thought in itself. To not want *anyone* to suffer is to accelerate your spiritual development and to awaken in greater degrees, because it expands and opens your heart on even greater levels.

When we are sleeping very deeply and someone tries to wake us up, if they call to us softly, we may not awaken. They may even call louder, and even then we still may not hear. Finally they scream at us and even pop us on the head and then and only then do we awaken. That is what suffering does for many of us. No one wants anyone to have to suffer, correct? So our best bet is to be determined to not fall asleep once we have awakened. The key is to do all we can to stay awake.

There is no quick-fix new age enlightenment pill to prevent suffering, at least not that I am aware of. My suggestion is for people to constantly observe their breathing and to remember that Love is constantly moving in and out of them. Yet how many will actually do this as a regular spiritual practice?

This is where suffering becomes key! Suffering helps to remind us of what is really important. Everyone I know that has experienced deep suffering is very grateful for the so-called little things in Life. So, therefore, one of the keys to decreasing suffering is to be grateful for the so-called little things in life which become very huge things once we know better. You know the things like our breathing and our heart's beat—**and let's not forget each other**. Look at all of the recent natural disasters. They definitely caused great suffering. Yet we could have possibly prevented many of them or at least been more prepared, if we but loved each other more. The vibrational frequency of Love has the capacity to even calm tsunamis!

So, yes, of course we can prevent suffering —but *will we*? That is the question! There is no one right answer, but there is one solution—and that is to love your neighbor as you love yourself. The more we as a collective body of humanity value spiritual principles over selfishness, the less suffering there will be in this world. I hope that answered your question.

4) *You've dedicated this book to the man who shot you, and you thank him for helping to be one of the catalysts of your spiritual transformation. Do you have a relationship with Anthony now? Did you two become friends after you forgave him and then saved his life with your warning?*

Anthony lives eternally in my heart. I have not seen him in physical form since that day, but you just invoked his presence now with your question about him. When I want to communicate with Anthony, or any of my many childhood friends who died or who I am not in physical contact with, what I do is close my eyes and open my heart. Within me is where they all live, and I also live in them and in the heart of all beings. So, yes, I do have a relationship with Anthony right now and, yes, we did become friends—and all of this took place within my very own being. This is how I have learned to perceive life. I had to, or else I would have gone crazy from thinking about all the people who were murdered around me as a child.

5) *You mention that it's not as effective to try to discover the leaves and branches of our Life Purpose before we have become aware that we ARE the root of it all. And I suppose once we've established a clear connection with the root, the leaves and branches naturally grow and reveal themselves to us, and we're led to what we need to be doing in the world. But, in the meantime (while we're waiting to awaken and realize the root), how do we choose to spend our time, or what to do for work?*

Focus on your breath, say thank you to Life as much as possible, find someone who needs a hug, and look at your baby picture as often as you can. All those simple things lead you to the root. Stop creating some reality in your mind that separates you from the whole. Saying things like, "what about us non-awakened people?" does not serve your highest good in any way. What it does is gives you a complex and expands your ego. Search your heart for the types of thoughts that place us all on the same level and connect us, like remembering that we all came forth out of the same source. It is true that we may be at different levels of awareness, and a steady and grounded income is important, but even in that, we all breathe the same air don't we? We all have eyes, ears, a nose, etc. We all want to experience bliss and true Love. Create more space within your heart.

Becoming more aware of the good that you are, with or without being emotionally attached to the details of your purpose, is what establishes the root. If you are working very hard so that someone else can live his or her Life Purpose, instead of complaining about that, see and affirm the beauty and goodness in your offering. Could helping them attain their Life Purpose be your Purpose? People oftentimes believe that they are not good or significant unless they are doing something extraordinary. We are good first and foremost simply because we are God!— or God's Children, or manifestations of God Consciousness, or whatever works for you. Not God in ego, but God in Love. Every action done in Love is indeed extraordinary! The more we realize this, the deeper the roots of our Life Purpose become. I have to remind myself of this all the time.

6) *We all know there are some things we can do that are compassionate—volunteer to help the homeless and hungry, offer comfort to an abused or neglected child, donate to worthy causes, and so on. But some of those activities take more time and*

energy than people who are just getting by have to spare. What are some things everyday people can do in their normal day-to-day routines and lives to help grow their compassion (or, to have more realization of the compassion they already are)?

Learn to first be more compassionate to yourself. That itself is a great attainment. In this day and time you can always find someone right inside your home that is hungry for your love. It is also very important to accept and embrace that we have much more capacity to give of ourselves then we realize. Mothers have proven this for thousands of years. And, by the way, we are all "everyday people."

7) *If you could go back in time and talk to the younger Temba—the one who was experiencing the abuse, the homelessness, the drug use, the gang violence—what would you say to him? Would you tell him about how his outlook would change, and that he'd find forgiveness and love? Or would you hold back, knowing he needed to go through that suffering in order to figure it out for himself?*

I do not know. Whatever has happened has happened. I cannot change the past nor do I want to. Everything that has happened has led me to this moment with you. I love you.

8) *What's one piece of advice or wisdom you can give to people who are still "seeking"— who haven't quite been able to realize or stay connected to the love 24/7 yet? Is*

there anything they can "do" to "get there" faster?

First we have to delete this "24/7" stuff. We all do our best in each moment. And also it does not serve your higher good to compare your spiritual growth to anyone else's. That comparison is what has given birth to this unreal concept of 24/7. Just relax and start appreciating your life more. Live each moment as if it was the last one you had to Love your family , humanity and Mother Earth.

Are you willing to spend more time with your own breathing, which is the very thing that sustains you? As I said, many people want the "Drive-thru #2 Enlightenment Happy Meal," and there is no such thing. Look at your baby picture every day, all day if you have to, and remember the innocence, beauty, and love that you were then and are still even now. The more time you make to practice, the more you will experience this thing that you are calling 24/7 spiritual experience.

Love, Temba Spirit

Chapter 9

Compassion is Your Nature

"If you want others to be happy, practice compassion. If you want to be happy, practice compassion."

—*Dalai Lama*

"The whole idea of compassion is based on a keen awareness of the interdependence of all living beings, which are all part of one another, and all involved in one another."

—*Thomas Merton*

"The dew of compassion is a tear."

—Lord Byron

Caring for another human being is a natural characteristic of humanity. There is nothing special about being compassionate. It is simply who we are. When you cut your finger, you treat it with compassion. You do all you can to nurture and heal it. You bandage it, and if it is a child's cut, you may even kiss it. You don't think about it. You just do it. That means that compassion is your nature and that it is nothing special. It is just who you really are.

If you saw someone bleeding to death on the street, your heart would be moved by the power of compassion. You would care about the stranger who was hurt. You would feel his or herpain. That is because compassion is your nature. It's nothing special. It's just who you really are.

The same would apply if there was a homeless child in front of you begging to be fed. Would you not do all you could to feed that child? Would there be anything more important than that? Would missing the train and being late for work matter if you were right in front of that beloved homeless and hungry child? Of course it would not. Why? Because compassion is your nature! It's nothing special. It's just who we all really are.

Why?

So now let me ask you a question. There are millions of starving children throughout the world, correct? Even in the supposedly wealthy United States of America, there are over 1.5 million homeless children. Wow! If compassion is our nature, how can something like this be? Why is it that in Los Angeles, New York, Detroit, Chicago and every other major city right now, pedestrians are walking by droves of homeless elders seemingly senseless to the fact that those people could be their parents? How can it be possible that America has millions of homeless elders and children if compassion is our true nature?

Now do you want to hear something deep? This is what Mother Teresa said out of her own precious lips before she transcended:

"When we pick up a man and give him a piece of bread, we have already satisfied his hunger. But if you find a man terribly lonely, this is a much greater poverty. You can find Calcutta all over the world if you have eyes to see. You can find people that are unwanted, unloved, uncared for, rejected by society, completely forgotten, and completely left alone. That is the greatest poverty of the rich countries."

Please contemplate Mother Teresa's words deeply. For years I have contemplated Her words and the power of compassion revealed something powerful to me. I would like to share it with you. Mother Teresa has presented us with a greater opportunity than we may realize. Check this out!

A Great Opportunity

On the opposite side of the scale of spiritual poverty is spiritual abundance. All we have to do is let the spiritual pendulum swing! Why stay stuck in the muck and mire of how material and selfish America and other rich countries have become? The entire world knows this. Let's be moved with compassion and turn the statistics upside down! With all of our hearts we have to embrace the power of solution! No more staying stuck on the thought of how selfish we have become. We can glance at the situation in order to remain aware, but let's all agree not to stare at it? Okay?

We are faced with a great opportunity! No one reading this is okay with any country having millions of homeless children and elders, right? If my heart is not okay with it, no heart is. We are all connected. We are all one!

And I am not saying for you to limit your compassion to just assisting and empowering the homeless. Compassion is an unlimited power. There are many areas in which the power of compassion can be applied. That specific answer will emerge once it becomes important enough to you. It indeed has become important enough to you and that is why you are reading this. I trust this with my whole heart and I believe in you. I am telling you, the solution to all the world's current woes is not just compassion but **your compassion.**

Hug Someone Today

The next time you see a homeless elder on the streets who you know is lonely, broken and has been abandoned by this cold world, take a moment to acknowledge them. And don't do this just for the homeless, but make it a spiritual practice to speak directly to the heart of everyone you encounter. *Especially those in your home.* Find somebody and hug them as if there were no tomorrow. **Please do not wait for a natural catastrophe to occur to exercise kindness and concern. Hug someone today simply for the sake of love and to expand the consciousness of compassion on this planet**. The power of your compassion will fill your heart and it will overflow. You can and you will drown the egos of this world in the ocean of your compassion.

Make a commitment to show affection to someone each and every day—including yourself. And don't limit yourself to only being affectionate to people. Go hug a tree or gently pet an animal or plant. The helping hands you are looking for are on the end of your own arms. Use them to hug yourself if it is you that needs a hug. Do unto life as you would want it to do unto you. Be as golden as the rule itself. Compassion is indeed your nature. It's nothing special. It's just who you really are.

Don't Deny Yourself the Experience of True Love

Do you work in a big city? Here is a good suggestion. The next time you go on your lunch break, treat someone homeless to lunch. Look this person in the eyes and say, "I love you." It is a total misnomer that every homeless person has psychiatric issues and will not be receptive to human affection. **Any journey that begins on the road of excuses will never be completed.** Treat them as you would want to be treated if you were in that situation. And as I said, look them right in the eyes. When you do this, you are looking into the very heart of God. You are doing unto others as you would want them to do unto you. Shed a tear for someone hurting. Tears of compassion have the power to moisten the hardest heart. The heat of your love can thaw out the coldest heart of any situation. **Compassion is your nature!**

There is a very good reason why all the Spiritual Masters who have walked this earth have told us not to forget the poor. The poor are the ones who help us the most to be moved with compassion. Compassion is what helps us to dive deep within our very own hearts. When we see someone dying, hurting, hungry, homeless, lonely, or suffering in any way, our hearts *effortlessly* open up. Is that not the goal of all spiritual practice? Do we not all want our hearts to stay open?

Please understand that when we share our Love with the poor and needy, it is we who are the true spiritual benefactors. *We* get to be moved with compassion. *We* are blessed to genuinely experience the very power of unconditional love. The people we share our love with benefit greatly as well. They get to know that someone truly does care. **That someone is you. You feed them food, they feed your heart. You give them a home; love makes your heart its home. You share your finances, you become spiritually rich. Exercising the power of compassion is a win-win for all.**

Being Spiritually Bankrupt Is a Good Thing

This is why I say that we in America have such a great opportunity. Because we have many more material distractions to overcome than most other places in the world, when we do overcome those distractions (and *we will)*, our characters will have developed true spiritual depth. For that reason alone am I proud to be an American!

You see, we here in America are the spiritual poorest of the poor. We are at the bottom of the barrel when it comes to spirituality—which means we also have greatest potential to inherit true spiritual depth. The deeper the dig is for the diamond, the greater the appreciation for it. The rarer the precious metal, the more value it attains.

We are that diamond that is way down deep in the coal of life waiting to emerge. And we are that precious metal waiting and wanting to be spiritually valued. And that's a great thing!

Some of us are in denial about this country's spiritual poverty, but why be, when there is such a great potential to become spiritually rich? **What an insult it is to put a monetary amount on how much you are worth. I am telling you, even if you are worth a trillion dollars in the eyes of the world, that is cheap in the eyes of love. In the eyes of love you are priceless!** For those of us who are willing to be brutally honest with ourselves and ready to discover our true wealth and also that beloved priceless treasure within—grab your shovels of compassion and let's start digging!

We can indeed Lead the World in Spiritual Richness

Love, nature, and our choices have placed us in the position to potentially lead the world in spirituality and true spiritual wealth. When the principle of compassion leads us, we will lead the world! Each one of us who has been able to develop spiritual character in spite of all the material distractions created by western culture can celebrate and claim the victory!

People on the spiritual path have admitted for years how hard it is to "be spiritual" in America. They have bragged about their trips to the exotic lands of the East and said how things were so spiritual "over there." All that may be true and is definitely a very beautiful thing, however, there is something just as beautiful that is being over-looked. Because America is the champion under-dog when it comes to spiritual richness, I know that Divine Love is rooting for it to reign victoriously where inheriting compassion is concerned!

And as certain people continue to affirm, decree, declare and maintain the status quo that there is a great challenge and difficulty to attain spirituality in America—little do they know, by doing so, they are also affirming that those who have *not* traveled to exotic lands, yet have still been able to develop spiritual depth, are people who are examples for the entire world to follow. **In fact, to be able to develop great spiritual depth while living in a society that is spiritually broke is the greatest of compliments.** The Power of Compassion revealed all this to me.

That woman in a 12-step meeting who lost her children because of her addiction but got them back because of her sobriety, who has been in prison but is now free, who was once a prostitute, yet now counsels women and walks through life fearless and with a huge smile of gratitude on her face, is the spiritual wealth of America and this entire world! She is the spiritual poverty of America transmuting itself into spiritual legacy and prosperity. She is something for the world to celebrate and honor!

And what about the person who has worked hard all his or her life, finally became a millionaire, and then lost it all? That pain is an internal pain that many of us cannot come close to understanding. Just ask all the people that committed suicide when the stock market crashed. I applaud all those people that chose Life instead. Sure, that person lost it all—but hitting that deep bottom made him or her emerge with a new appreciation for life and a new and improved spiritual depth, awareness and courage! With this new attitude, approach to life, and spiritually rich character, such a person is now moved by the power of compassion. He or she may set out once again to gain material riches, but this time the motive is filled with an unfeigned love for humanity. He or she once again does become financially wealthy, and now they lead the community in humanitarian projects and charitable causes.

And what about my dear friend **Marcy Cole,** Ph.D., who just launched **"CMomA"** (Childless Mothers Adopt 501-c3) a non-profit explosion of love and open hearts that offer support to childless single women and couples who seek to adopt children in need of a safe and loving home. Imagine the opportunity to fulfill the parental dreams of countless individuals by nurturing and empowering so many orphaned and abandoned children to live a fulfilled life through this beloved vision. This is now a reality and the ripple effects of gladness will be endless. Check it out and Join the Force of Good: www.CMomA.org

We Will Embody Compassion

These people and the many other waves of compassion that make up the great ocean of humanity's Love, are something to be honored, adored, appreciated, and celebrated. They are spiritual examples for the world to follow. They and the millions of other people that have dedicated their lives to the service of this world make me proud to be a human being. America and the rest of humanity will only be truly transformed when we all join hearts and hands and embrace and exercise the power of compassion. This great move first begins within our hearts—yours and mine. **In this most precious moment, I adore and celebrate you, beloved friend. I know with perfect confidence that you truly care. Compassion is Your Nature. It's nothing special, it's just who we all really are.**

The heart of this world will indeed embody compassion. We are on that path now. Those who are spiritually sensitive enough know this to be true. **The thing that is least expected to happen will indeed happen! The underdog will come out victorious. This is always how it happens in the spiritual world.**

America is not the "big Sataan" as some extremely religious folks would have us believe. America is Divine Love's lost and prodigal child. We are not a government or society of greedy and selfish people. **We are simply— "The People."** Does this sound familiar? Everyone knows that we have our share of issues, but it is high time to let that go and to visualize and affirm and apply the potential US (U.S). We are collectively a conscious body of energy that is awakening and unfolding into greater degrees of Innocence, Beauty, and Love **and Yes—Compassion.**

Your faith has to become perfect and unshakable! You have to know that the power of love and compassion that is in you alone is strong enough to sustain this country—and the rest of the world for that matter!

"As long as I am here, all of the rest of us will be okay." This is what you must tell yourself. This is a powerful shift of awareness. "Divine Love has its eyes on me and I am in this world. All is fine and all will be fine. There are no worries." This is the attitude of the spiritually rich!

As a country and a world we will hit a very deep bottom. That is because it is the destiny and Life Purpose of humanity to develop great spiritual depth and character. This entire world is indeed headed for a spiritual bottom. The inner worlds of many of us have already hit that bottom, so the great transformation and awakening is already occurring. So many of us are fed up with the old status-quo of selfishness that we have embraced for so long. Hitting a bottom is a good thing. When all is lost, we become open and we develop true empathy.

When this collective opening occurs, we will then be receptive enough for true spiritual brilliance to consume us. Once Compassion saturates our collective consciousness, then and only then, will we truly be a United States and also a United world. Everyone has this potential destiny. This reality is available for all who choose to exercise the unlimited and inexhaustible power of compassion.

Governments will fall and man-made systems will crumble, however, **"We the People"** will embrace with our entire hearts, minds, and strength, the eternal principles and qualities of Innocence, Beauty, and Love and therefore live forever.

Now, beloved friends, go find someone to hug who really could use one. That person could be you. Be moved by the boundless and illustrious power of compassion.

I Love and adore you so much. Temba Spirit

Temba Spirit Bio

Ever since Temba Spirit put his life on the line by renouncing his gang affiliation on national television (A&E, History Channel), he has devoted his life to service, spirit, love, and helping others to **Reclaim Their Power**.

After an early life that included child abuse, gang violence, drugs, homelessness, depression, and incarceration, Temba underwent an amazing spiritual transformation while behind bars at Rikers Island prison. With support and inspiration from Amma, the world-renowned hugging saint from India, not only did Temba fully forgive himself, he transformed his prison time into a spiritual retreat. He initiated a meditation program, distributed spiritual books, and did all he could to help the hurting men who were incarcerated with him to re-awaken their spiritual innocence— showing them by example and through his actions that love was inside of them and there was nothing they could do to change that, no matter how heinous their crimes. Now, over a decade later, the program he started for these men, *Circle of Love Inside*, has spread all over the U.S. and has become one of the most successful prison outreaches of our time.

Temba's amazing journey of love has led him to join with an array of famous book authors, transformational personalities, spiritual leaders, and celebrities. In 2007, he was discovered by Janet Bray Attwood and Chris Attwood, the New York Times bestselling authors of *The Passion Test: The Effortless Path to Discovering Your Destiny*, and since then he has shared a stage with Byron Katie (*Loving What Is*), Mark Victor Hansen and Jack Canfield (*Chicken Soup for the Soul*), Debra Poneman (founder of the Yes to Success seminars and a pioneer of the self-help industry), and Michael Beckwith (featured in *The Secret* and founder of the Agape International Spiritual Center).

Marci Shimoff (author of *Happy for No Reason*, who has sold over 14 million self-help books) says of Temba: "Temba has been a great inspiration to me, as he is a wonderful role model of service and love toward others. In fact, I respect Temba so much that I interviewed him for my book *Love for No Reason*. He is one of the 150 'love luminaries' I interviewed about unconditional love (along with top scientists, psychologists, subject matter experts, and spiritual teachers) and Temba's was one of the most wise, profound, and moving of all the interviews."

Along with Temba's spiritual and humanitarian work (including his creation of a program to empower and support a Native American orphan family in the poorest area of the country, the Pine Ridge reservation in South Dakota), he has also had success in music as a conscious hip-hop artist, performing with the legendary KRS-ONE, considered by many to be the greatest conscious lyricist of all time. The song he wrote for Janet Attwood at the behest of Michael Beckwith, **Reclaim Your Power**, has become a favorite of thousands at motivational seminars all over the country. He has even performed at a gathering for President Obama hosted by Louis Gossett, Jr. in Beverly Hills.

Temba sees his music, inspirational speaking, book writing, and humanitarian work as one mission— different yet related ways in which consciousness is expressing itself as love. Despite his painful beginnings, Temba's life has become a powerful expression of service to humanity. As he puts it, "I have taken the crap of my life and turned it into spiritual fertilizer!"

Temba Spirit is available for speaking engagements, interviews and performances. Please email for more info.
tembaspirit@gmail.com   www.tembaspirit.com

Made in the USA
Lexington, KY
02 November 2012